# PUSH THROUGH

## Release Your Past and Step Into Your Divine Destiny

Dr Jacqueline Njeri Samuels

**Push Through: Release Your Past and Step into Your Divine Destiny.**

Copyright © 2018 by Dr Jacqueline Njeri Samuels. All Rights Reserved. Revised August 2020

No part of this publication may be reproduced, distributed, or transmitted in any form or by any means, including photocopying, recording, or other electronic or mechanical methods, or by any information storage and retrieval system without the prior written permission of the publisher, except in the case of very brief quotations embodied in critical reviews and certain other non-commercial uses permitted by copyright law.

**Bible References:**

Scripture quotations marked ESVUK are from the English Standard Version Anglicised © 2001 by Crossway Bibles.

Scripture quotations marked NIVUK are from The New International Version® Anglicized © 1979, 1984, 2011 Biblica, Inc.®

Scripture quotations marked NKJV are from the New King James Version® © 1982 Thomas Nelson.

Scripture quotations marked NLT are from the New Living Translation © 1996, 2004, 2015 Tyndale House Foundation.

**Other References:**

https://en.wikipedia.org/wiki/Languages_of_Kenya

**Learn more at -**
https://bit.ly/GratitudeStarterKitFREEdwnld

## Dedication

I dedicate this book to every person who has known fear, desperation and confusion.

If you are actively searching for true love and meaning to your life, this book is for you.

Finally, I dedicate this transformational journey to every determined Superstar who's pushing through obstacles to move into your new season. You are a work of art. Prepare to be moulded into the masterpiece that is your true identity as you embrace your truth and release through these pages.

With love and deepest gratitude for the opportunity to touch your life.

Jackie

# Table of Contents

## Table of Contents

**PUSH THROUGH** ..................................................................i

Release Your Past and Step Into Your Divine Destiny..........................................................................i

Dr Jacqueline Njeri Samuels ............................i

Dedication ............................................................... iii

Table of Contents.................................................... iv

Acknowledgements ............................................. viii

Foreword ................................................................ xi

Preface: Obedience to Birth This Book.............. xiii

Part 1: Inexperienced Start In Life ........................ 1

Chapter 1: Welcome to the World!.................... 2

Music All Around ........................................... 3

First Dance ...................................................... 3

Young Talent Emerges ................................... 4

Primary Life: First Taste of Live Performances........ 5

Chapter 2: Early Career Path Defined ............. 7

Music Learning and Teaching Career ........... 9

An Embarrassing Performance Freeze-up ... 11

Chapter 3: Life is a Stage ................................ 15

The Mystery of Change................................. 18

Mom's Provision Through Loss ................... 20

God's Saving Grace .................................................. 22
Opening Doors for My Musical Gifts ...................... 23
Chapter 4: Start of the Dark Night ............................ 27
Costly Change of Plan ............................................. 29
The Punching Bag Escapes ...................................... 34
Where's the Gold in the Tragedy? ............................ 37
When Menacing Relations Strike ............................ 41
3 Attitudes that Sabotage Confidence ..................... 45
1. Cultural dominance ............................................. 46
2. Transference at work ........................................... 47
3. Acting 'Macho' before one's friends .................... 48
Dealing with Contact Objects ................................. 52
Prepare for Repositioning to a New Assignment ... 55
Part 2: Learning the Faith Walk .................................. 57
Chapter 5: The Power of Waiting in Faith ................. 58
Releasing Prophetic Faith ....................................... 62
The LORD Our Protector ....................................... 64
Be Fully Poured Out ............................................... 65
Chapter 6: Dealing with Injustice and Ill Health ...... 69
Guarding Your Heart: A Life Lesson ...................... 73
Chapter 7: Speaking and Doing .................................. 77
The Power of Decisiveness: Learning to Say 'No' .. 80
Busy-ness or Rest? .................................................. 81
Stillness and Listening ............................................ 84

v

Decision Making and Timing .................................. 85
Chapter 8: The Message of Hope ........................... 91
    Embrace the Power of Making Right Choices ........ 94
Chapter 9: Creativity and Doing Good ..................... 98
    God's Goodness ....................................................... 102
    How are You Sharpening Your Gifts? .................... 104
Part 3: The Inner Healing Process ............................. 105
Chapter 10: Embracing Peace in Relationships ....... 106
    Understand Cultural Backgrounds and Communication Differences ................................... 106
    What's Love Got to Do with it? ............................... 110
    First, What Love Is Not… ........................................ 110
    Second, The Fragrance and Character of LOVE .... 111
Chapter 11: My True Love: ........................................ 116
The Answer to Mom's Prophecy ............................... 116
    Shifting From Fear to Faith .................................... 120
    Unhealthy Fear-based Childhood Incident .......... 122
Chapter 12: Where Faith Meets Miraculous Healing 125
Chapter 13: Being Aligned to Your Destiny Helpers 128
    Destiny Helpers #1: MA, Readjustment after loss 130
    Destiny Helpers #2: Mom's Prophecy Realised ... 132
    Destiny Helpers #3: PHD Studies, Mom's Passing, Family Transition ..................................... 133
    Destiny Helpers #4: 2nd Marriage, Birth of 2nd Son ............................................................................. 135

Peter Weds Jackie: Highlights .................................138

Chapter 14: Timing in Showing up in the Now ........141
  Find Your Gift and Voice in Every Day Experiences............................................................143

Chapter 15: Empowerment for the Mission Ahead..147
  Letting Your Light Shine .........................................150
  God in My Future ...................................................152

Chapter 16: Don't Take the Safe Path; Push Through into Your Divine Destiny ..........................154
  Final Thoughts: You Are A Vessel of Hope ...........156
  Appendix 1: My Story Shared in Kenyan Tabloids 157

# Acknowledgements

Since it's not possible to fit everyone who has been instrumental in nurturing my physical, spiritual and emotional health and wellbeing, God bless you all for pouring into my life and investing your love, time, resources and prayers with faith. I am indebted to the following who have walked this profound journey with me:

**The Holy Spirit:** Without Your guidance and constant walk and gentle nudges I would not be here today, and this book would not exist. I am so grateful that You always confirm Your Word – faithful to the end You are! I honour, love and trust You.

**My wonderful husband and soul mate Peter:** Thank you for showing me what true love is all about, for believing in me and releasing me to live out my true calling. Surely, delayed is not denied! I'm eternally grateful for our daily walk in the garden of self-discovery, love and honour. You are the answer to our Moms' prayers and my heart's cry. I love you deeply, my Precious friend and life companion!

**Edy and Jonathan:** My wonderful miracle sons. Along with your dad Peter, you have been the best gifts to me. May the LORD daily direct your footsteps as you grow in love, grace, wisdom, peace and unity, pressing forth into your divine calling. Grow into the champions God created you to be as new doors of favour and abundance open up for you to push through in every season of your precious lives. Always seek out the best in others and be the change makers, following the path of peace, love and faithfulness. With all my love.

**Sammy and Annie Mwangi:** What can I say? I'm forever grateful for your immense love and compassion, patience and unrelenting faith in me. You taught me that God could turn my story around. You believed in me and renewed my hope when few others would look my way or listen. That's why it is with immense pride and gratitude I call you my 'kinsmen redeemers'. I love you dearly my 2nd parents. May our Redeemer daily bless the work of your hands and continue enriching your precious family on every side.

**My brother Isaac:** Your resilience, quiet confidence and wisdom have been my much needed fuel to push through especially through the darkest night when I needed your physical presence and quiet strength the most. Thank you for standing with me. I love you Aizo! May the LORD Almighty continue to guide, nourish, direct and empower your precious family.

**My siblings:** I am grateful for the family we belong to. Your kind words and timely showing up through my life's changing phases has been such a blessing to me. May your light continually shine in your spaces as you bring hope to others in your sphere of influence.

**Washington and the Late Leah Muuya:** Thank you both for giving me life. You never gave up on me even when I faltered. Thank you for encouraging me to pursue my musical gift and nourishing my spiritual walk. I will always love you.

# Foreword

Since the moment our Volvo cars met and fell in love at the church service where we first met back in February 2002 it has been a joy, honour and pleasure to become Jackie's soulmate, prayer partner and co-minister in the work of the Lord. Having been through a previous failed marriage relationship I had been carrying my own hurts and fears for many years, but our wonderful Lord and Saviour, Jesus Christ, has a miraculous way of joining broken pieces together to make a new whole.

Jackie has a lot of class and is able to relate to people of high status. She has an infectious sense of humour and relates very naturally to indigenous people in the UK. She is also an effective teacher and communicator. I sometimes feel she is more English whilst I am more African! However, whilst we were courting, I remember thanking God that she shops at Primark!

I cannot forget praying with Jackie's auntie whilst on a mission to Kenya at Easter 2002 with tears stating that I only wanted to become involved with Jackie if it was the Lord's will. We have always sought to put the Lord first in our lives together. Our marriage has been a journey and a blessing to my life. Although we are both far from perfect, God has given us a special grace to love and bear with each other.

There are many gifts and talents in Jackie's life, some of them were always visible, such as her singing and piano playing, whilst others have taken time to surface or resurface. One of them is writing this book which has coincided with the Lord opening doors for her to minister and share her life story. Whilst many of these opportunities have been at ladies' meetings I have on occasion been blessed to experience her ministry and observe the fruit of touched and changed lives.

The writing of this book has also been a cathartic experience for Jackie. Although it has been a sacrifice to release her to spend many days and evenings writing, often late into the night, I believe the sacrifice is more than worth it for the many lives that will be changed through the reading of this book.

I wholeheartedly recommend this book to you, especially if you have unlocked hurts in your life. The Lord whom Jackie, I and our household serve is real: He cares about you too and wants to mend your broken pieces and put your life back on the right path. May He minister to you as you read this book. May He enable you to fulfil your full potential and reach your God-given destiny.

With love and blessings,

Rev. Dr. Peter Samuels

Petra Church (UK)

# Preface: Obedience to Birth This Book

This book is a direct response to the voice of the Holy Spirit who instructed me two years ago to write a book detailing some of the most painful and life-changing experiences that have taken place in the first half-century of my precious life. The book's title was birthed from much prayer and meditation. 'Push Through: Release Your Past and Step into Your Divine Destiny' details my journey from despair, self-searching and self-discovery.

Life is filled with choices we each have to make on a daily basis: to obey or ignore an important instruction that could be the one button positioned to change the trajectory of our lives. Oftentimes we find ourselves choosing fear over faith as we give in to the negative voices knocking about in our minds rather than turning these fears into the fuel to excel and craft the future we're capable of and deserve.

When we ignore the inner warning signs that constantly flash in our space, we hold ourselves captive thus disabling the move of greater power from stepping in to assist us to overcome and push through to embrace our God-given destiny. The realisation that we are never alone in the journey is the key that will propel us forward to discover who we were created to become. Every step moves us closer to our ultimate position. Is a delayed response synonymous with denial? This is a question that plagues many, myself included, leading to wrong turns that embellish life further.

When people, situations and time collide in perfect harmony they can orchestrate a beautiful reality called LIFE. In this book you'll learn how I've taken the lessons learnt from my past and used them to propel me into a new reality, with a deeper compassion for others who find themselves in a similar plight.

If someone was sent along your path to help your healing process, would you recognise them or just ignore them as you walked on by?

With so many questions I came to the edge of the mountain top and looked down at what lay before me – a shattered life, a confused mindset, broken hopes and dreams, the pit of utter despair - with seemingly no way possible to take my first step without falling into the deep abyss.

Still that quiet Voice whispered to me: 'Jump in. I'll catch you and guide you through this journey. The light is only visible on the other side of this tunnel.'

Hesitant at first, I jumped in. Amazingly, I didn't sink. *'Great'*, I thought to myself. *'I wonder if I can take the first step now? What will happen if...'* and so the journey began.

It is my sincere prayer that the key life lessons learnt, along with the thought-provoking questions raised in this book will ignite the reader to dare to dream, hope and believe again. May you be encouraged to activate your God-given voice as you release the mistakes of your past and ultimately embrace your divine calling with confidence, love, joy and daily gratitude for the second chance you've been accorded.

I invite you to walk through the tunnel of self-discovery and healing with me and together let's find the light on the other side... It's time for a real, lasting breakthrough. Finally. Are you ready for the ride?

God bless you as you embrace this message of hope and share it with others to help them to push through and step into their divine destiny.

With much love and gratitude,

Jackie Njeri Samuels

# Part 1: Inexperienced Start In Life

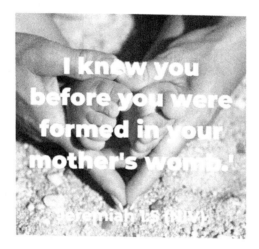

## Chapter 1: Welcome to the World!

Born in the mid '60s into an average middle-class working family, I was the youngest of three children for the first six years of my life. Shortly before my 6th birthday my younger sister Mary joined the world. Closely followed by our youngest brother the following year, just two days after my seventh birthday. With five siblings in the family, life was busy for our parents. With our birthdays being so close together my younger brother Isaac and I have typically enjoyed joint birthday celebrations. This has created a special bond where we look out for one another.

During my first decade of life both our parents were teachers. I recall Mom regaling us with stories of how she and Dad met: Dad was Mom's tutor at Teacher Training College where she was studying to become a qualified teacher. After lectures she and Dad would often meet up by the shops for a discreet chat. In those days dating in public was frowned upon and children couldn't just bring home a friend of the opposite gender. One had to be sure of the intent to marry before introducing an intended life partner to their parents. This expectation made its way into our family as we grew older.

Dad in turn shared how he was studying in Washington DC, USA during my birth. He and Mom had decided that if the baby was a boy they'd call him

John after the then US president John F. Kennedy. In the event the baby turned out to be a girl, they'd call her Jacqueline after President Kennedy's wife Jacqueline Onassis. When I came along they named me Jacqueline (or 'Jackie' for short).

## Music All Around

Growing up our house was surrounded by music. Both my parents loved to sing and dance at home. Dad's bass rang out cheerfully complemented by Mom's soprano. I remember my parents dancing to famous pop songs of the day. When they were in high spirits they'd play 'Mister Walker' or 'Jane' on the turntable, sing along and dance in step to the beat. An African classic was 'Kweli Musa', whose lyrics and rhythm I still find amusing. This song is part of the 'zilizopendwa' – the well loved oldies from back in the day. Sometimes my parents would have friends and neighbours join their parties. On such occasions we children were usually allowed to stay up later than normal, as long as we stayed out of sight in our bedrooms. However, as curious children we sometimes sneaked downstairs to watch the dancing scene and tried not to giggle too loudly.

## First Dance

I recall the first time Dad took my older siblings and me to a dance. As we were all in separate boarding secondary schools at the time, we only met up during the school holidays. Hence going dancing with a parent was an unexpected offer to be grabbed wholeheartedly.

When we arrived at the party venue there were a few children about our age who we didn't know. After a while Dad asked me if I wanted to dance. While I sat there wondering if Dad was going to ask me to dance with him, along came this very tall fellow who I'd never met before. He looked about my Dad's age, hardly my age group. He politely asked Dad if he could dance with me and I was whisked off to the dance floor. What was meant to be a waltz or some fast music turned into the most hilarious dance session of my life! My three steps equalled one huge stride for this dance partner. We looked so silly my siblings and other onlookers were roaring with laughter! My embarrassment turned into laughing gas as I'd never been placed in such an awkward position before. To my relief the song eventually ended, at which point I made myself scarce for the longest time after. I didn't want to be co-opted into another dance with a total stranger. Thankfully, I've never had to endure a similar experience since.

## Young Talent Emerges

Although I'm not sure when Dad started singing in church choir, I remember him belting out Christmas carols as the season approached.

I recall two of my favourite musical moments in my first decade of life. The first defining musical moment began at about five years of age when Dad placed me on his lap and taught me to play the well known 'Joy to the world, the Lord is come' on the accordion. At the time I had no clue what the notes were. Dad was a great accordion teacher. He enthusiastically showed me how to play the white notes descending from treble C all the way to Middle C. As my tiny fingers skipped and glided across the white notes, Dad continued to encourage me. As I got the hang of the note sequence he then added some bass notes with his left hand. The harmonies he played must have imprinted themselves into my memory as years later I was able to play the song on the piano and work out the harmonies without reading staff notation.

## Primary Life: First Taste of Live Performances

My older siblings and me attended Lavington Primary School for seven years, The School had many teachers from the UK, being one of the top primary schools in Nairobi at the time. Music was an important part of the curriculum. For several years we also attended Lavington Church we learnt many songs in Sunday School.

We also took part in Christmas and Easter time plays where we were typically given various acting or singing roles. I remember one Carol service where I was chosen to sing a solo in the first verse of a famous Carol 'Praise to the Lord, the Almighty; the King of creation' in a foreign language. The words have stuck with me even though I don't speak the language. I guess I was destined to be a witness of the goodness of God through music as it was being woven into the very fabric of my tender life from an early age.

# Chapter 2: Early Career Path Defined

It came as no surprise to the family when I chose to pursue Music as a main subject in secondary school. At Kenya High School where I did my 'O' and 'A' Levels, we had music specialists come in to teach us. My favourite music teacher was a Peace Corp volunteer from the US named Ms Mary Cole who joined us for a few years. Ms Cole had a strict marking scheme in her highly engaging piano lessons. With her high expectations, if one had not practiced for a single day Ms Cole would sometimes give students -10/40! After receiving this horrendous grade once, I quickly learnt that daily practice was a must if I wanted to achieve anything worthwhile in my musical life.

Ms Cole's teaching was geared towards creating a well-rounded musician who felt and interpreted the music. This resonated with my personality as I was always to be found in the music room experimenting with new tunes and harmonies of the songs we were learning in class and at choir. Ms Cole's motto was to always try our best, and failing was not an option. Being immersed in this competitive environment as a youth taught me to always seek out ways of improving my skill and improve my talent.

I remember a disgusting incident when I was climbing up the stairs to practice piano in the Music room at school one rainy morning. I'd decided to skip breakfast in order to make a head start on a tricky piece ahead of my piano lesson scheduled for the first period. On the third stair I suddenly slipped on something slimy. As my step faltered I screamed in fright, simultaneously reaching out to steady my balance. The Music room was opposite the Art room. The Art teacher Mr Okanga rushed out to find out if I was alright. I looked down at what slipped on. 'Yuck!' I shouted. 'I stepped on a snail and nearly landed on my face!'

'What's wrong, are you hurt, Jackie?' he asked.

'*No! But I hate snails*!' I yelled back at him not realising how ridiculous I sounded. Mr Okanga broke out in his signature hearty laugh. He tried reasoning with me that it was just a snail, but I was having none of it. I remember then hobbling over to the toilets and lifting up my right leg to the sink to wash off the disgusting slimy feeling from the ball of my foot. The more soap I applied the worse I felt. I felt sick to my gut and eventually dried my foot and headed back to the Music room, watching my steps very carefully this time.

See how having a passion for something can cause such a fracas? The key is to persevere even when you are inconvenienced or don't particularly enjoy the journey, like I did.

## Music Learning and Teaching Career

My parents were keen to encourage us to harness our musical talents. I recall when I was due to sit for my 'O' level exams Mom announced that she'd buy me a keyboard if I got good grades. This was the incentive I needed to work even harder. I set to work with the mindset that I'd be the best in my class. You can imagine my joy when I discovered that I'd achieved the highest Music grades in the entire country! With my Music Distinction my parents honoured their word; I received my first shiny new Technics keyboard for Christmas. Oh the joy of creating real music from the comfort of my home! Meanwhile, my older brother and sister got new guitars. It was great having a home band of sorts. I don't recall our younger siblings being given a similar educational challenge at this point as they were still in primary school.

While my older siblings learnt accompaniments for the upbeat songs they learnt at their Church youth sessions, I was busy working on mastering some classical harmonies and creating fancy accompaniments, utilising what I'd been studying at school. In July 1980 I took the Associated Board of the Royal Schools of Music (ABRSM) Grade 5 piano and voice exams and passed with Merit. I committed to studying and passing the higher graded levels in the years that followed. After my 'A' Levels where I also attained top marks nationally, I joined the part-time staff at the Conservatoire of Music, before joining Kenyatta University (KU) to further my musical studies.

While completing my Bachelors Degree at KU I continued teaching students what I'd learnt and guiding them through the ABRSM music curriculum in music theory, piano and voice. My highest student Gacigi Kungu attained a Diploma in Piano performance and Grade 8 in voice. They went on to complete a Bachelor's Degree in Music Education with 1st Class Honours at Kenyatta University and now serve at a private international school in Nairobi.

It's humbling to know that all the students I entered for ABRSM, GCSE and other exams have passed. Many have gone on to create successful lives in their chosen field, some as far afield as USA, Canada, Europe and various parts of Africa. I'm grateful to be the person entrusted with the task of watering these talented seeds as they took targeted action on what they learned.

During the course of my music teaching career I have encountered different learning styles and preferences among students of all ages and walks of life. One of my favourite tips to unlock new learning involves applying simple strategies for learning passages of music by heart. By applying what's worked consistently for me I'm able to help others create similar success in developing individual performance techniques. For instance breaking down the trickiest passages found in more technically challenging pieces has proved to be most beneficial in quickly developing finger dexterity and seamlessly connecting two contrasting sections of music within a larger work.

There's no greater feeling of satisfaction and gratitude than watching students' faces and body language relax as they push through what previously appeared to be an insurmountable challenge, to finally overcome the fear of getting a tricky passage right on a continuous basis. Add to that the confidence exuded when performing the whole piece in public. That's gold!

## An Embarrassing Performance Freeze-up

I'm sharing my first public embarrassing performance with you to show you that fear of the crowd doesn't have to cramp your style or amazing gift & talent.

At Kenya High School music students were encouraged to take part in public musical performances both within the school and local community. We took part in choral ensembles, instrumental and vocal solos, duets, trios and quartets. We also joined up with local boys' schools for mixed choral performances, mainly with Lenana and Nairobi Schools. I remember when in Form 3 (the equivalent of Year 9 in the UK) I froze up on stage as I was about to perform a Grade 4 piano piece at the national Music Festival in Nairobi, Kenya. The venue was the famed KICC amphitheatre in the heart of the City. This was my maiden public solo instrumental performance in front of a huge crowd of strangers. As I looked up at the audience I felt knots start to tighten in my belly; stage fright taken a hold of me.

Suddenly my vision blurred as I looked around the packed amphitheatre where hundreds of expectant eyes were looking down at me, waiting for me to unleash my musical talent. Alas, when I looked down at the grand piano before me, I could not make out the notes! I'd suffered temporary visual blindness right there in front of all those students, teachers, parents, and adjudicators! What on earth was going on?

As if sensing my agony, the crowd waited patiently for me to start as the adjudicator rang the bell a second time... and a third ring shortly after... 'It's now or never' I recall thinking to myself.

Somehow I found my voice and whispered in desperation to my music teacher who had come over to encourage me to start, 'Where is 'D'? The teacher reached out and played 'D' for me. At once my vision and memory returned and I placed my hands in the same starting position I had practised so many times before. The notes of the 'Rondo in G' piece started forming and were soon flawlessly executed while I shut my eyes and just let my fingers to their thing.

This was the power of muscle memory at work! This was the moment I had studied so hard and practised faithfully for 6 months for! This was my moment of truth. And it paid off! There was a roar of clapping going on around me. 'I've done it!' I thought. My relief was tangible as I staggered back to my seat to join my school mates.

When the performances were over, the adjudicators read out the results. They simply mentioned how unfortunate it was that I had hesitated for so long, otherwise I would have been placed among the top 3 positions. However, they felt that to be fair to the other performers they had to penalise me. I lost some points and was placed 4th overall, which didn't bother me. I was just glad to have made it through that first excruciating national performance in the presence of hundreds of expectant onlookers.

I'm happy to say, there's been no repeat performance of that fateful 'mental freeze' or panic since. I am so grateful to have learnt how to counter my nerves when performing by practising special breathing exercises to reset my focus and calm my nerves.

The last 3 decades have been spent teaching students how to overcome panic attacks, master pre-performance nerves and focus on improving muscle memory in order to face any performance challenge with confidence, grace and the right mindset. Preparation is key.

Having been in the public speaking arena for a while now, I realise that nervous attacks are not foreign to public speakers, instrumentalists, vocalists, dancers, sports people or anyone who is charged with a gift to share their skill in public. The secret is to prepare yourself, learn how to focus on the task at hand, practice your craft or art in order to improve and perfect your skill and talent. Constantly focusing on being prepared and taking targeted action to turn your desire for excellence in execution into a reality takes work and dedication.

# Chapter 3: Life is a Stage

All the world's a stage, and all the men
and women merely players;
They have their exits and their entrances,
and one man in his time plays many
parts, his acts being seven ages.

Excerpt of a poem by William
Shakespeare (1564 – 1616)

As children we start out with little knowledge. As we approach teenage, we suddenly shift to thinking we know it all. By the time we hit our early twenties it's *'Surely our parents are stone age, what do they know about this life we're living? What can our parents teach us? I can do this on my own. I know better than anyone older than me. Why should I listen to my elders? Just leave me alone!'*

And so the saga of little - and bigger - mistakes begins.

When we reject the wise counsel of our elders, we're opening ourselves up to the School of hard knocks to take on the role of the all-in-one trio of 'teacher, judge and jury' who are happy to chastise us with little thought given to the consequences of their harsh actions.

On the other hand, when we choose to listen to the voice of reason and wise counsel from our parents and elders, we gain much respect. We are cushioned in the true love that reflects the character and heart of our Creator.

Every person's journey through life is individual to them. Each one's character is largely shaped by their life experiences, the love – or lack of love – that surrounds them, and the words spoken in their presence. Without proper guidance much time is wasted wandering through the streets of broken dreams, insecurity, false hopes and an endless spiral of wrong turns. Is there any point in moving on, any point in looking for a way out of the wilderness in which we sometimes find ourselves? We wonder who we should cry out to for help, release and inspiration. How do we articulate the feelings buried deep within the soul, and who should we trust?

These are all pertinent questions that plagued me for a long while. The answers in every situation were found within and around me. As a musician and educator, former actress and lifelong student of life, my life has indeed proved to be a stage where the players are lined up in tune with the particular scene being enacted. How one scene ends and another unfolds in every life is largely dependent upon the individual's perception and understanding of it, along with their reactions while in that scene.

Indeed, life is a stage where the orchestra sounds the harmonies or discords that blend with the action taking place. Every member of the orchestra is responsible for playing their part to the fullest extent possible to ensure harmony is realised. However, when the chords are sounded out of synch the resulting cacophony is deafening to all around! Like the choral or orchestral conductor, the dance choreographer is charged with the unique responsibility of ensuring harmony is attained and maintained throughout the performance. Allowing loose ends to remain unresolved can end one's career prematurely.

You may have heard that what happens to you is not as important as how you react to what happens to you. Have you tested this phrase recently? I have, and the result is this book. I've done my best to describe the events that have stood out for me in various scenes of my life's stage. Although some of the key players in every scene are different, there is a thread that holds the whole masterpiece together, ensuring that growth is taking place at every turn.

And that's life my friend. The journey of self-discovery begins when you say 'yes' to allowing the pieces – both the ugly and the good - to show up at their accorded time. When you commit to being open to growing and you allow yourself to become vulnerable through the process, that's when the real change begins on the inside. Pressing through is mandatory for real change to be wholesome. It's important to remember that once you start the change process there is no turning back, especially if you desire to live a fulfilled life of empowerment and impact.

In the past two years I tried many times to overcome the urge to write my story. The result was restlessness, and a feeling that I was short-changing myself and those who needed to hear my message. I believe that everyone who reads these pages has something waiting to erupt from deep within, they just need that initial push to get started. The key to applying the Law of Motion in the process of change lies in creating the momentum to keep the wheels turning to ensure the growth event fully materialises.

The Law of Motion started in my life by putting pen to paper and journaling some pivotal moments that have helped shape my life. The more I penned the greater the urge to write. Eventually I started typing it all up and the momentum was created.

## The Mystery of Change

As we grow older the journey of life takes on new twists and turns. Some turns propel us towards our destinies; others move us further back from our intended goals. While many major shifts in our lives as adults are the result of decisions we've personally made, others are the after effect of experiences beyond our control. A broken marriage often leaves children stranded in a situation not of their making.

The feelings of rejection and unworthiness may lead to self-blame. If left unaddressed the resulting anger can have devastating effects on the youngster.

Once loving parents may shift to indifference, fall out of love with each other, or end up being disconnected for whatever reason. The carefree family fabric is compromised and once again the children are often left to fend for themselves and seek out love and comfort from other sources outside the immediate family. Way too often the parents are so busy nursing their personal wounds that they fail to notice the subtle shifts happening to their vulnerable children whose once perfect world has started to fall apart and they don't know what to do about it to make it better. If there is a formula for recognising when change happens in the various stages of our lives I'm yet to find it.

Somewhere during our early teen years I began noticing a subtle shift taking place in our family network. Although we were well provided for materially, our parents' work conditions sometimes took them to distant locations. As a result all five siblings were shipped off to boarding school. The only time we met up was during the holidays. During this time Mom went to study abroad in Finland, Israel, and Tanzania. When she returned from Finland Mom brought me two piano books featuring Finnish Christmas carols. Interestingly, over 20 years later someone at work blessed me with a CD of Finnish Carols! As the Christmas season approaches we fish this CD out and sing along as I remember my dear Mom's thoughtful action with gratitude.

While mulling over the mystery of providence in our lives I recently heard that when the student is ready the teacher will show up. This statement may also apply to specific provision being made available when the need arises. This can be a lifesaver particularly when dealing with difficult situations as we'll discover in the following example.

## Mom's Provision Through Loss

There were several instances Mom had to steel herself from the numerous challenges that she endured when we were growing up. Yet through the trials she never complained.

Mom had been away studying in Tanzania for a few months. My four siblings and I had just returned home from school that evening, being the start of the four-day half term holiday. While we expected to spend the holiday with Dad we were pleasantly surprised to find Mom at home ready to welcome us with a hot meal and lots of cuddles. She'd secretly taken the weekend off from her training in Tanzania to be home with us that weekend; this move turned out to be a divinely pre-orchestrated.

We were sat at the dinner table talking about our recent school experiences when there was a knock on the door. Upon answering the door I was asked to take a phone call at our neighbour's house as our phone was not working. One of Mom's younger brothers had called; he sounded strangely withdrawn as he asked to speak to his sister. I hurried back home to fetch Mom who got up excitedly and rushed over to the neighbour's house to answer the call.

I'll never forget the look on Mom's face when she returned from the neighbour's. That look of horror, utter disbelief and shock - all intertwined on her face. We asked her what was wrong and she just said, 'He's gone' as the tears slowly made their way down her beautiful face and onto her clothing. This was a quiet tearful anguish that I had never before witnessed on her. When eventually Mom was able to share with us what had happened to Uncle Zachary, we all started weeping.

Every sibling is precious, and for Mom to imagine no longer being able to laugh and share family jokes and life experiences with her sibling was beyond comprehension. We all loved Uncle Zachary's family and had spent many meaningful weekends together. Both he and his wife aunt Tabitha were school teachers, and during our many visits they had given me some much-needed tuition.

I'm convinced that Mom's request to have that particular weekend off to spend time with us was actually the Lord's divine intervention and providence. I am grateful that although Mom was not present for her brother's send off the following week, she was able to make peace with the incident because she was in the country at the right time.

Indeed, blood is thicker than water. As the first born in her family my mother helped her father in bringing up all her younger siblings after their mother passed away in the 1950s, thus making her loss akin to losing one of her own offspring.

The following verse from Psalm 61:1-2 (KJV) encourages my spirit when the agony of overwhelm seeks to challenge my inner peace:

Hear my cry, O God; attend unto my prayer.

From the end of the earth, will I cry unto Thee.

When my heart is overwhelmed: Lead me to the rock that is higher than I.

**Prayer**:

Thank You LORD that whenever I am feeling overwhelmed You remain my Strong Tower, my Rock and my Deliverer. Help me to hold on to You, my only source of healing and restoration, for You are my help in time of need. I know that You will always lead me to a place of safety and teach me to smile and laugh again. Amen.

## God's Saving Grace

My family started worshipping at St Andrews Church when I was in mid-primary school. Sunday School was fun with lots of acting opportunities in skits and musicals. My favourite was 'Joseph and the technicolour dream coat'. I remember performing it with the Brownies and Scouts one year. Later at Phoenix

Players when we performed the longer version Ian Mbugua and I were narrators and vocal trainers.

When I moved to Kenya High School we had a kind Chaplain who doubled up as our Religious Education teacher. We also had regular visits from the St Andrews Church ministers. In my 2nd form during one of Reverend George Wanjau's visits and spiritual exaltations I gave my life to the LORD. Something Rev. Wanjau shared about the love of Jesus struck a chord in my heart. I realised I was a sinner and needed the LORD's help in my life.

At home life had changed. Being in boarding school I learned through discussions with friends that our families came in different flavours, from all walks of life. Since most girls were not prepared for boarding life beforehand, our House Matron took on the role of 'second mother' to the students in her care in our home away from home. As young teenage girls we needed an adult to confide in as we weren't allowed to phone our parents during the school week. Phone calls and family visits were kept to a minimum and were only allowed at weekends. Our default position was to tuck away any questions and to embrace our present lives in the best way our young minds could cope with.

## Opening Doors for My Musical Gifts

I'm grateful for the time I spent learning Christian music and gaining spiritual guidance at St Andrew's Church Choir Nairobi for over 2 decades. In the late

1970s-80s I sang soprano alongside my headmistress, Mrs Margaret Wanjohi, with my Dad's bass voice booming behind me as the lilting 4-part choral harmonies wafted through the choir stalls to trumpet trills from the towering organ.

This daunting experience taught me many useful life keys – from respecting our elders (being one of the youngest choristers alongside my schoolmates), honouring our LORD and Creator through worship, to working together in a spirit of unity, love and commitment.

At School these musical talents were often put to the test. I was made Chapel pianist and School pianist in the early '80s, alongside the late Lydia Achieng' Abura. Performing solos, conducting and accompanying songs gave me the courage to perform in larger groups. As my talents grew, so did the hunger to train others around me to excel in Music. The resulting success of thousands of students I've had the absolute pleasure and honour to impact musically speaking has been nothing short of a miracle.

It's profound how the musical skills gained have over the years opened various doors to me. To name a few: St Andrew's choir was among 14 choirs selected in Nairobi in 1978 to form the first Kenyan National Mass Choir; I was among the choristers. From performing with St Andrew's and other well known choirs for the President and other dignitaries at State House Nairobi and beyond, I've also conducted, accompanied and soloed in the Nairobi Music

Society, the German Choir, the Muungano Choir, Kenya Posts & Telecommunications (Nairobi) Choir (KPTC), and been part of the panel selected to revise our Kenyan National Anthem in Mombasa in the early 1980s.

I was also honoured by being contracted to work as the Music Consultant for the KPTC (Nairobi) Choir during the Biennial Eistedffod Music Festival in South Africa in 1995 where we brought home numerous medals, right after acquiring more at the National Kenya Music Festival.

My role as a National Music adjudicator led me around many Provinces countrywide, later travelling to other countries including France, South Africa and the UK to share my musical gifts in the diaspora.

Whilst co-directing choir with Ian Mbugua at St Andrews I also somehow found the time to start the Kenya Conservatoire Choir, a venture that has been continued by two of my former students: Gacigi Kungu and Cynthia Mungai. For all these opportunities I am eternally grateful.

I believe when you allow the Holy Spirit to guide your path, at whatever age, and say 'Yes' to allowing your gifts to shine through, your doors will be opened to you. This has been my reality as a former Music Lecturer at Kenyatta University, Music coach, artist and author currently based in the UK where I graduated with a Doctorate in Music and Special Educational Needs.

My mission is to continue to actively impart to others the skills and knowledge that I've gained in a bid to unlock the doors for those who are actively asking, seeking and knocking for their opportunity to shine through.

However, in the following section you'll learn how my spiritual and emotional journey has been anything but smooth. The potholes and confusion that followed my saying 'yes' to following the LORD nearly swallowed me up, but for the grace of God...

# Chapter 4: Start of the Dark Night

Before I share the toughest story about this dark season of my life and what led to the choices I made, I urge you not to judge. All I ask is that you hear me out as you reflect on what you would have done had you been walking in my shoes:

After my first degree I met a young man who appeared very sweet. He was a Muslim while I was a Christian. This should have been the first warning sign not to get closely entangled with him. However, since he was funny and happened to know some of my Christian friends, I figured he must be a good guy. I was not serious about getting married as I was busy following my dream: choirs, lecturing, adjudicating, acting and performing gigs.

The guy got serious and asked to meet my family. I eventually agreed and took him to meet Mom at her office as Dad was very strict about bringing anyone home, and I wasn't about to be humiliated in front of the guy. Mom was more diplomatic in dealing with us. If she didn't like a situation she'd tell us why in a caring manner (sometimes with some chastising too). Although we didn't always see eye to eye on everything, on this one thing both my parents were right. This man was clearly not the one for me.

As we got up to leave her office, Mom spoke to me in vernacular asking, *'What are you doing with him?'* I responded, *'It's not like I'm marrying him, Mom!'* At this she flatly told me to stay away from him. When left her office I tried to brush off her words. I guess my emotions were already tangled.

Within a few months my response to Mom would be seriously tested. The man started pressing me to marry him. Knowing what my parents felt about him I hesitated agreeing immediately. When I finally agreed we started arranging the customary parents' meetings for both sides of the family to meet up. At this point Dad got furious and categorically refused to attend, forbidding Mom in the process. Mom however made up her mind that she would stand by me against his will. Dad would often fight Mom whenever she attended these introductory meetings. The confusion going on hurt a great deal. Once I asked Mom, *'Why doesn't Dad want me to marry this man?'* Why's he fighting you for attending the meetings, why doesn't he want to attend yet you've both been invited?'

Mom's frank response surprised me: It went something like this:

'You are my daughter, Jackie. I gave birth to you. I love you. I will stand by you even though I don't think this man is right for you. Don't worry that your Dad's not here. I will stand by you.'

So in this hostile environment we put our wedding plans on pause.

## Costly Change of Plan

I have often wondered why I went against my parents' wishes by going ahead and marrying my first husband. Could it be that I wanted to prove a point? It turned out to be much more than that.

Something happened after we had been courting for about a year. Dad saw that I was not letting go of this man, so he organised for me to be married off to someone else – worse, someone he'd vetted at a bar during one of his drinking sprees. I never got to know if it was one of his friends. Here's how I got to know of the plot:

We had just finished choir practice at church when one of my distant aunties called out to me: 'Congratulations on your pre-wedding meeting on Saturday.' Not realising my aunt was actually addressing me I didn't respond but kept on walking down the steps towards the car park.

Auntie wondered why I was not responding, and reverted to vernacular, addressing me by my home name: 'Njeri, why are you ignoring me? I thought you are happy about your wedding. Why haven't you invited us, or is it meant to be a secret?'

I was in shock when my auntie called out with these questions! Up to that time I had absolutely no idea of any such plan! Further questioning my aunt for details of what she was alluding to also revealed some unsavoury details about this guy. It turned out this was Dad's idea, and Mom had no clue… I headed straight for my parents' home from choir practice and demanded to know what was going on from Mom. Mom expressed her shock and horror at the news and vehemently denied having any knowledge of the plot to marry me off... I stormed out of my parents' house with one resolve...

Guess what happened next?

In foolishness and retaliation, upon discovering my Dad's plot to marry me off as a 2nd wife to a 40-something year old stranger I'd never met, I decided to go ahead and get married secretly to my suitor in order to escape the arranged marriage. We were married the following week on Mom's birthday.

Imagine the shock when I presented Mom with my new husband on her birthday, complete with a birthday cake for her, and a wedding cake from us?! Sorry Mom! If only I could just turn back the clock...

**Key Lessons**:

a) *Never underestimate the power of your words and actions.* Our words truly have the power to heal or to destroy, to restore or to condemn, to bring hope or to snuff out the last ember of hope and faith in another's life.

b) *Watch the people you allow yourself to be surrounded by.* Wrong connections create soul ties that are hard to break. Soul ties can set you off on a journey you never dreamed of embarking on. Allowing yourself to be tied to the wrong person comes at a very costly price...

In my case, the retaliation was a lifeline... one I've ended up paying dearly for when it could have been avoided had I chosen to simply listen to and obey my parents instead of rebelling against their wise counsel. Is that why they say 'love is blind'?

There are a number of suggestions I want to leave with you from this bearing-my-heart story:

1. *Never judge a book by its cover.* Listen to the wise counsel of your elders. They probably know something you don't, although the way they share their knowledge might not always be desirable or resonate with you.

2. *Seek first to understand.* If in doubt, WAIT before committing to an action. This is especially relevant as pertains to making important life-changing decisions and choices that affect other people. Avoid plunging into a pit by being hasty in your actions or reactions or prepare to face the consequences.

3. *Not all relationships lead to marriage.* Not everyone is marriage material for you. Don't allow peer pressure to rule your decision-making process either.

4. *Own up to your mistakes, humble yourself and ask for forgiveness from those you've affected by the decision you've taken.* I had to swallow my pride and ask my parents for forgiveness in time... a most humiliating experience, but so releasing at the same time.

5. *Forgive yourself when you err.* Remember that we are all fallible in this life. Imperfection is part of being human. If you don't forgive yourself you won't be able to move on in any meaningful way. Unforgiveness also keeps you from embracing your greatest life and attracting what you're really worth. Remember what you don't make room for can't come to you.

6. *Be gracious when you see others making a silly mistake that you can see but they can't.* It may well be that they are too emotionally involved to see the dangers and possible pitfalls ahead. Instead of blaming them or talking nonsense behind their back, warn them in love and gentleness.

7. *Hold back.* Time is a great resource that helps clear the inner eyes of perspective and enables logic to play a crucial part in the process. Heed the warning signs you see when you're about to make some potential life-changing decisions. Pay close attention to the warnings of those that genuinely care about you and your welfare.

8. *Seek spiritual guidance in all important decision-making processes.* Yes, divine intervention shows up in unexpected ways. Remember, the God of second chances wants to give you a beautiful future. If you do end up in 'hot soup' like I did, it's not the end of the world (even though it may well feel like it at the time).

9. Sometimes the LORD will remove the stumbling block from your path because the path He

has outlined for you does not include the person or persons you have chosen to walk that path with. That's what happened in my case, as I discovered after my first husband met his demise in a tragic car accident.

10. *Finally, look for the lesson in the challenge.* Seek to improve your decision-making process by utilising the lessons learned so that in future you will be wiser and will endeavour to exercise greater care if you're ever in a similar situation. Also use what you learn from the experience to empower others.

While praying for revelation and understanding of the reasons behind the drastic action outlined above which caused real havoc in the lives of those connected to me, I was reminded of a Scripture in Ephesians 6: 1-4 that addresses both children and parents:

Vs1: Children, obey your parents in the Lord, for this is right. "Honour your father and mother" (this is the first commandment with a promise), "that it may go well with you and that you may live long in the land."

Vs4: Fathers, do not provoke your children to anger, but bring them up in the discipline and instruction of the Lord. (ESVUK)

As I considered why I'd reacted in such an uncharacteristic manner following my aunt's questioning on that day on the church steps, Verse 4 of the above passage of Scripture immediately stood out to me. I suddenly realised that my actions were really a cry for help. It is my sincere prayer that this will never happen to you, your offspring or anyone else known to you.

As a parent now, whenever I sense that I may have pushed my children too far, I consciously purpose to back off and give them some slack as I can't imagine them going through such humiliation. To the parents: may the Holy Spirit help us to become good stewards of the responsibilities He has entrusted to us as we bring up our children in the discipline and instruction of the LORD.

May we correct our children in love and compassion, gently admonishing them when they stumble, for surely love covers a multitude of sins.

## The Punching Bag Escapes

Shortly after I got married to my first husband, he turned me into his punching bag and started systematically stripping me of my confidence and self-worth, defiling my mind and body. He'd taunt me and ask me to do things I did not believe to be right. When I refused he'd beat me. This went on for months.

He also got his younger brother and cousins who he'd brought over to live with us to turn against me. One day his younger brother was told that he had the 'authority to discipline me' if he thought I needed it. Imagine a full-grown woman being told I was not worth defending myself or worth being respected by someone eight years my junior! To top off the insult, I was also paying school fees for my brother-in-law.

Unfortunately, since my parents had been against our marriage from the start there's no way I was about to report what was happening in my marriage to them.

This Muslim man who while we were courting would sometimes meet me at church to drop me home after choir practice showed no hint that he didn't like me attending church. All that pretence changed once we were married as he suddenly forbade me from going to church. When I disobeyed him he'd sort me out with his fists and vile tongue insulting my Creator. That drove a deep wound into my soul as I loved worshipping the LORD with the like-minded choral team.

One weekday the man arrived back from Mombasa where he was working, opened the front door and ran up the stairs to our bedroom where I was. As I started to speak he silently lifted me up in the air as if I was a child. In a wild rage he ripped one shoe off my foot and proceeded to smash my face from side to side with it. In the process he dislodged the bridge I had on my left lower jaw. The pain was excruciating! I stumbled to the window while screaming for help at which point he hit me again as he yanked me away from the window. By now neighbours were peering out trying to see who was crying out for help.

Later I learned that the reason he had beaten me that Wednesday night was because he'd been told that some man had dropped me home the previous day. A previous time I'd been chastised for allowing my older brother to give me a lift home. When he learned this time it was two female University colleagues who'd dropped me off, he didn't believe it, so I got a beating.

At this point I decided I'd had enough of the abuse. I was going to find a way of escaping this hostile environment when it got dark and head to my parents' home a short distance away. While he slept I packed my bags and at the crack of dawn the following morning I grabbed my bags, quietly snuck out of the house and ran all the way to the back of my parent's home. I climbed the wall to their compound through the neighbours' patch; they loaned me a stool to step on. In my haste and fear I just threw my bags over the wall.

Mom was already making breakfast in the kitchen and she watched silently as first my bags landed on the ground shortly after followed by me jumping over the fence. Taking one look at my swollen black-eyed face Mom scurried upstairs to wake up Dad. Dad was furious with the man when I related what had happened to me the previous night. Moreover, he wanted to go smash the man's face, but both Mom and I stopped him.

It was 12th December, a public (bank) holiday. I was due to perform at a national event followed by dinner with the President and various other dignitaries at State House in a few hours so I gingerly got dressed and headed there. This cruel tyrant of a husband was surprised to see me appear live on the telly later that day as I accompanied the University choir on the piano and sang a trio with the two colleagues who'd dropped me home the previous night. Later, while he waited for me to return home I was nowhere to seen. It's sad that I was too embarrassed to tell my friends the truth about how I'd incurred my injuries.

Being through with the abuse, I'd decided to travel to Mombasa where we had our second residence (also where he worked at the time). After consulting with Mom, the day after the performance I travelled back and forth through the night by coach to clear my belongings from that house as I didn't intend to return there. I remember the coach driver, Mzee Ali, asking me about my black eye in a very concerned tone. This was the same driver who often transported me to Mombasa. With the coach full that evening, Mzee Ali offered me a seat in the co-driver's seat, right at the front of the coach where he promised to keep an eye out for me. Although I tried to dodge telling him the truth about how I'd obtained my injuries, he wasn't fooled.

We arrived at the coach terminal in Mombasa about 3.30 in the morning. Mzee Ali offered to wait for me at the terminal while I headed over to the house by taxi at that hour. I quickly threw my belongings into some bags, made my way back to the bus which got me back to Nairobi shortly after. The driver kindly dropped me off at my parents' home.

## Where's the Gold in the Tragedy?
Believe it or not, there can be some gold hidden within, despite our present afflictions. In my case,

the change happened through a series of events and tough decisions on my part.

My parents were distraught at my plight. After I returned from clearing my stuff in Mombasa I needed some time to recover. Meanwhile my parents organised a meeting between both families. My husband was confronted and made to publicly apologise to me and my family for mistreating me, in the presence of both sets of parents and grandparents. When his father started insulting my family to his family in their Nandi language, my grandfather fluently spoke some words of wisdom to them in their language which surprised them as they had no clue any of us understood their tongue. I had previously witnessed dad-in-law rough up his wife for something menial. Granddad told them that he had never laid a finger on my grandma and they had lived peacefully for nearly 60 years at that point. Granddad believed no one had the right to physically abuse another person, no matter what they had done. I agree with him.

Once I'd calmed down I chose to forgive my husband for the physical abuse and humiliation of the past year. I'm pleased to report that he started treating me like I was valuable after that turnaround meeting.

It was during the healing process that I got pregnant with our first child. However, the LORD warned me in a series of dreams that something nasty was about to shift my entire existence. Just 3 days after my 28th birthday in July on his way back to Nairobi from Mombasa, my first husband died in a tragic motor accident along with two other colleagues. The horrendous incident was covered by the tabloids who periodically started sharing my story. His death changed the trajectory of my life. I'll share some of the difficulties that followed shortly.

Sometimes all it takes for one's life to be completely overhauled is a single life experience... whether good or bad. Life can never be the same after such an incident occurs. The best thing that came out of this dire set of experiences was the birth of my precious son Edy. It's amazing that God saw fit to grant me – a disobedient child of His – this special gift. Perhaps to restore some much-needed hope within my spirit and to shine His loving light upon me and my family. I believe the LORD was letting us know He was still on His Throne while all these nasty things were happening around us.

**What lessons have you learned from your difficult experiences?** It's important to ponder the following thoughts in order to resolve any dormant issues in your life that may have held you captive and unable to move on.

**Ask yourself if something happened in your life that has changed your perspective of life.** For instance, there may be people in your life that have spoken damaging words to you or about you. As a result you may have started believing those words and devaluing yourself.

**You may be closing yourself off from accepting genuine love and care from others.**

Perhaps you feel as though you don't deserve to be loved because your life is in such a mess right now.

When you start to feel wanted and cared for, you might find yourself pushing those feelings away mistakenly believing that you're undeserving of such affection. That is a lie from the enemy designed to keep you trapped.

Have you been struggling with diminished self-confidence and self-worth as a result of a past experience? Do you have a 'victim mentality', or have you blamed others for what's happened in your life?

**Do you constantly wonder if anyone will ever truly love you and accept you as you are?** Have you stopped grooming yourself and allowing yourself the gift of looking, feeling or smelling desirable? If any of these resonates with you, rest assured there is a way out.

***Remember that your present situation does not have to define your future reality.*** There needs to be a mindset shift before you can start to embrace your new life and begin to live life on your own terms – a life that is both desirable and amazing. That's the life you were brought into this earth for, it's what you truly deserve.

In the next section we'll examine some of the attitudes that instil fear and anxiety in people, and how to reverse these negative feelings in order to start creating a more harmonious life that allows you to thrive and hope again.

# When Menacing Relations Strike

> Even though I walk through the valley of the shadow of death, I will fear no evil, for You are with me; Your rod and Your staff, they comfort me.
>
> (Psalm 23:4 ESV)

Have you recently passed through a deep tunnel in your life where all you see is darkness around you? You may be feeling lonely and helpless thinking you've no-one to share your inner anguish and pain with. Perhaps you're struggling with devastating thoughts of giving up and ending it all, crying *'What's the use of carrying on anyway?'* as depressive thoughts play with your mind, threatening to take control of your life.

I can understand your anguish, my friend. I've been there. I've felt these tormenting feelings at various points of my precious life. There were moments when I was close to losing all hope. I cried endless tears while wallowing in self-pity. It felt like there was no one who could understand the depth of my pain, sorrow and bewilderment. Even family members had no clue how to console me despite their best efforts. Being left pregnant and widowed at only 28 years of age was unknown territory for all around me.

During the 23 months we were married, his erratic behaviour towards me had turned the love into fear. My self-esteem took a sharp nose dive after my first husband's tragic accident, due to some very painful incidences that followed shortly after. In my confusion and inner turmoil I began shutting myself away from those who tried to reach out to me. In the process of writing this book I now realise that I had emotionally closed a certain door in my life, just to be able to face each new day.

It's strange how people who are cruel to us can have such a hold on us, even after they are gone from our lives.

Within hours of my first husband's demise, his family started hounding me and emotionally battering my family. This started shortly after we informed them of the accident. While we travelled to the mortuary in Machakos, some in-laws travelled to my house and started turning my house upside down. We returned to my house after midnight to find my bedroom ransacked. When I enquired who'd done this my house-help said my sister-in-law had been in there searching for a title deed for a plot of land we'd been given by his parents as a wedding gift. There were more unwelcome visits in the months that followed where these former in-laws stole personal effects from the house while I was out at work or at rehearsal.

My son was born four months after his biological father passed on. Sometimes I would take my baby with me to rehearsals and performances as I was worried about his safety. Since my responsibilities also involved evening performances and travel abroad I'd sometimes leave my son in the care of my parents when I was working away.

On one occasion my former father-in-law and an 'uncle' arrived unannounced at my house with some uniformed army men in an army van. The group proceeded to terrorise our watchman then made their way upstairs to my flat and knocked on my door. As soon as the house-help opened the door the men proceeded to push her down the stairs as they made for the door with my four-month-old son. I was out at choir rehearsal at the time.

By the grace of God my baby was reclaimed by my younger brother Isaac who had moved in to live with me for increased protection. My brother heard the commotion from the kitchen and calmly came into the living room to find my son in the arms of one of these awful men. My brother calmly told them that I was not in as he took my son into his arms, and asked the men to come back when I was in since they said they had come to see me.

The men eventually left, annoyed that their plan hadn't worked, only to return exactly two months later, during the day. This time I was in the shower and heard my house-help whisper in a scared voice through the door, 'Auntie, they are back'. Even as I asked her who she meant, in my heart I already knew who she was referring to. She confirmed it.

I have never summarised a shower and got dressed so quickly in my life! Like a shot I dashed into the living room, grabbed hold of my baby who was now six months old. We ran into the bedroom and I locked the door securely with a key. I asked my house-help not to let them in. I needn't have worried about that. There's no way she was going to open the door to these tormentors after what had happened to her the last time!

While we were hiding in the bedroom I received a phone call from my neighbour downstairs informing me that she had seen a number of army clad men walking around the compound. She said under no circumstances should I venture to open my door to anyone until she phoned back to confirm that they had gone. The day watchman was also nowhere to be seen. Eventually, these uninvited guests got tired of knocking on my door and left us alone. I am so grateful for the evil men's foiled plans through our caring and godly neighbours' quick actions.

There was a kiosk (small shop) a few yards from our house. The kiosk owner later informed me that he had been watching the events taking place in my compound and had cautioned the local watchmen including ours to be on the lookout. He said he had seen certain members of my late husband's family hanging around our street over the past few months since his passing. They had been watching who was coming in or leaving our compound.

It was scary to learn there were informers posted outside our compound whose sole purpose was to spy on us. No wonder they seemed to know when to come and terrorise us and steal our stuff! Seriously, why would anyone want to take off with all my knives, serving spoons, wooden spoons, title deed, curtains and other personal items from my house? I sure have no clue! I suspected the man's family wanted to use these items as contact objects, and to do us harm. I say this because I'd learnt that some of the family members were into witchcraft. There were a few scary incidents my family went through with their family during and after the funeral…

**Word of warning**: Beware of who you interact with and who you trust.

## 3 Attitudes that Sabotage Confidence

In the last section we looked at how making wrong choices can have dire consequences in our lives. I shared one of my most tragic moments and how one decision I made that was fuelled by rebellion has changed the trajectory of my life for good.

In this section we'll examine some of the main blockages that affect our moving forward after life deals us a terrible blow.

You've probably met them: Some people come into our lives and dismantle the harmony and sense of peace that we've been enjoying right up to that moment. These people who once seemed so genuine, caring, gentle and soft-spoken suddenly turn out to be real wolves. They begin to systematically rip apart our sense of security and self-confidence. They find fault with every little thing we do. They start basically commanding our ship and telling us what to do. To add insult to injury these selfish folk never take our counsel seriously because in their eyes we have nothing of importance to say. Worse still, if we dare try to voice an opinion we'll be chastised – physically, verbally, emotionally...

Have you or someone you know gone through such a horrifying scenario? Perhaps a family member or good friend is going through this right now. If you're witnessing this, are you wondering if you should say something and risk becoming a target to the abuser? What's most likely happening if someone is towering over you or your loved one in such a threatening and demeaning manner?

I'll endeavour to share some personal insights with a few examples to help you understand the context of certain actions people sometimes take. Such decisions make absolutely no sense whatsoever from where you're coming from... ready?

## 1. Cultural dominance

An example of 'cultural dominance' mechanism at work is where the male is taught that they are the heads of the homes so everyone else [women and children] have no say. If the 'others' speak, they are punished for having an opinion.

It reminds me of the movie 'Ants' where Zee was told he could get into trouble for being seen to be listening in on a conversation. Imagine that! Perhaps you too were chastised because the person thought you had overheard something they were talking about that you clearly weren't meant to overhear!

I don't know about you, but this kind of thinking is so outrageous! And yet it does happen. More than we may realise. I remember in secondary school once being punished after being made the scapegoat for something that went wrong … worse still – I wasn't even there when whatever had happened took place!

It's a cruel world out there my friend! People are not always logical when they are making decisions or taking actions that affect others. It seems that the desire for self gratification and shifting blame often overrides common sense.

## 2. Transference at work

Here's a prime example: A man's parents used to fight when he was growing up… As the man grew into adulthood he learnt that he must fight his spouse in order to get some respect from his peers and to let people know who's boss. Ever heard the phrase 'like attracts like'? I think we should make an exception to this rule in this case, agreed?

## 3. Acting 'Macho' before one's friends

Let's use a fictitious character 'Ben' here. In this scenario Ben is showing off how 'macho' he is to his friends… Ben takes increasingly bolder action steps to humiliate and completely deflate his girlfriend or partner. In his mind Ben thinks he is looking good in his friends' eyes. In reality? His friends think 'Ben' is really stupid and what he is doing isn't appealing to them. However Ben's 'friends' dare not tell him what they really think about his behaviour for fear of possible repercussions to themselves. So Ben thinks he has 'bragging rights' because of that 'macho' feeling that boosts his confidence and makes him careless in his actions, attitude and perceptions. It may not be long before Ben makes a mistake that brings him back to his senses…

In today's world you may have noticed how people tend to move away from anything resembling domestic violence and humiliation effected in public. Even the law keepers will typically tend to stay away when one person is being mistreated. Growing up in Kenya I thought this only happened among the African communities. However, since living in other parts of the world I have since come to the realisation that physical and emotional abuse are not restricted to a single community or region. What's more worrying is that when the perpetrators' actions are not challenged, many people's lives are put in jeopardy as a result of negligence.

This makes it crucial to find a way to get some help if you or someone you know is going through some form of abuse that you know about.

While physical abuse is more easily recognisable, other forms of abuse are less tangible unless someone speaks out. Emotional abuse for instance can lead to self harm, increasing fear, anxiety and depression. If the root cause is not addressed the victim will continue to deteriorate and the end result may be devastating. The key is to identify and treat these negative feelings and symptoms in order to start creating a more harmonious life that allows one to thrive and hope again.

All these are symptoms of an aching heart that is in great need of receiving love. If the victim does not seek help to address the worry and anxiety that often result from physical, emotional, verbal and psychological abuse, they may end up depressed, just like I was for a season in my life after losing someone I cared about. Worse, if you allow yourself to sink low enough without getting any help, you may end up self-harming.

Thankfully, there is a way out of this dilemma. I have found prayer to be a great spiritual dose. It's important to realise that the physical and emotional parts of your whole wellbeing also need to be addressed and nourished, alongside your spiritual dimension. When we are ill we go to the doctor who diagnoses the problem. Doctors however, can only do so much to help an aching soul. Doctors are often treating the symptom, not the root cause.

It's therefore paramount to your healing and total restoration that you find the root cause of your pain, worry, anxiety or depression. Since illness and disease do not typically operate in isolation, by finding the root cause of your discomfort and illness you will be able to reverse and repair what needs to be dealt with. Thus harmony will be restored to you, making you wholesome once again.

When prayer is added to the mix, you are now addressing the whole person. Why pray? Prayer is the overall 'pill' – the fuel for the soul and the glue that gels together body, mind, soul and spirit.

I've had the privilege to meet plenty of people who've been delivered from bondages of various forms of illness – from physical, emotional and mental – all through the power of prayer blended with faith.

Shortly after my second son was born I was also delivered from a trophoblastic tumour. My uterus prolapsed four weeks after his birth. This was a very embarrassing and worrying time since until it happened to me I had no clue what a prolapse was. After months of trying to employ non-surgical means of repairing the damage to my womb with no success, the doctors finally decided to operate. During surgery the surgeons found and removed a lump that hadn't showed up in the X-ray taken before the procedure. Out came my uterus in the process. There followed MRI and CT scans to determine if there were any lingering surprises. Thankfully none were found. This was a miracle that was confirmed by three specialists. I thank God for my healing and restoration to health.

Do you have an illness you want healed? Ask the LORD Jesus for your healing without delay. Ask believing that you have already received your healing and it is so. All you need is faith like a mustard seed. Remember the woman with the issue of blood? Let's imagine she had spent a lot of money on doctors; they were unable to relieve her of the illness and the uncleanness that meant that she could not handle any object, sit on any chair or lie on a bed used by others without contaminating these items. Worse, in her unclean state this daughter of Abraham could not touch her loved ones or get close to her husband (if she had one) without making them unclean in the process. The Old Testament Law required all who were ceremonially unclean to wash themselves and their clothing, and still remain unclean till evening. All this was the woman's reality for 12 long years! You can read the Old Testament Law relating to dealing with uncleanness in Leviticus 15:2-13.

Yet, this precious child of the Most High God continued to believe that she could be fully restored. And so, when she heard that Jesus was passing by, she determined to just touch the hem of His garment and believed that she would be made whole from the affliction that had plagued her for 12 long years. The woman's unwavering faith made her whole. The same power that worked in her because of her faith in the LORD her Healer – Jehovah Rapha - is available to you and your loved ones today, my friend. Will you choose to believe God and receive your healing and restoration today?

## Dealing with Contact Objects

Don't just accept an object from someone who you have a bad feeling about. If someone offers you a 'gift' and you feel funny about receiving it from them, my advice is to politely decline the gift. There are many instances where my 'intuition' on this sensitive matter has paid off. Many years ago, I was offered some beautiful clothing that I eventually had to get rid of. Once I wore a certain pair of trousers I'd received as a gift from my first husband. As soon as I put on the trousers I suddenly felt as if strange animals were climbing up my thighs. To my horror and utter dismay, I looked down at my thighs to see these snake-like images of every colour on my trousers. Their shape was facing upwards. Anyone who knows me knows that snakes and I have nothing in common. Needless to say, those trousers were history within moments of that shocking discovery and experience. Ever since, before investing any money on clothing I've taken to checking the print or patterns very carefully. If in doubt I simply leave the item on the shelf or hanger and move away.

Another time I had bought some pairs of earrings with matching rings. Shortly after I went to church for a deliverance prayer meeting and as we were praying, we were asked to open up our fists with palms facing the ceiling. I tried to perform this simple action and strangely found that my fists were shut tight against my will. The pastor who was praying repeated the instruction to open my fists. I tried again to open them with no joy. No matter how hard I tried they simply wouldn't open. I wondered what was going on. It was as if some outside force was holding my hands in a tight fist.

The pastor who observed what was happening to me came over and took hold of my left hand where I wore two rings. As the pastor prayed over the third and fourth fingers of my left hand (where the rings were) he had a word of knowledge. He said that there was some strange power emanating from both the rings and from my earrings. He then commanded my locked fists to open which they immediately did. He then instructed me to remove the rings; I willingly obliged. The moment these items came off me there followed a prayer of release and disconnection from all manner of harm or negative effects connected to the objects mentioned. The peace that overwhelmed me was amazing.

The pastor also prayed for the Holy Spirit to reveal to me other harmful items that were hidden in my home that had been holding me captive to the power of the enemy. Sure enough, when I got home I identified other items that were tainted; I was quick to get rid of them all that same night. We set up a bonfire in the garden and burnt them all - not your usual bonfire though! Our Maasai watchman was intrigued by the whole episode and grateful for the extra warmth the fire provided him that cold night.

The above incident reminds me of a quote I read recently by Thaddeus Golas: "What happens (to you) is not as important as how you react to what happens."

As children of the Most High we often encounter

---

Ascribe to the LORD the glory due His name; worship the LORD in the splendour of His holiness.

(Psalm 29:2. NIV)

---

people who speak words of knowledge over our lives. These divine utterances represent the mind and heart of God who loves us dearly and only desires the very best for us as His precious children. For this reason, it is crucial for us to take immediate and targeted action on words of knowledge or wisdom nuggets shared with us to warn, protect, or rebuke us. Such quick action, when performed in obedience to the leading of the Holy Spirit, would act to diffuse any further adverse effects from following us or our families. Sometimes the healing and restoration are immediate; however, on other occasions it takes time. In either case, do not despair my friend if your breakthrough is taking some time to manifest.

I have shared some of these experiences at church conferences and prayer meetings where I have been invited to speak in various cities of the UK. It always amazes me how people later seek me out to share how my testimony has helped to free them from any number of oppressive experiences and bondages that had long held them captive. It is always humbling to witness the LORD's compassionate breakthroughs and manifestation of His grace upon the souls that submit to His healing and call to surrender to His restorative power. All glory and honour belong to the LORD our God!

When we honour the LORD and give Him thanks for His marvellous works, we unlock doors of more breakthrough and His glorious peace flows through us. The LORD Almighty is in the business of saving, healing, delivering and restoring even the most broken vessel.

## Prepare for Repositioning to a New Assignment

As you prepare to step forth into your divine calling trust that God who knows every detail of your life is able to guide you to your destiny if you simply ask Him. The key is to be willing to follow His leading, trust His timing, and be open to trusting that the people He brings your way to help you will not lead you astray. Too often we look to a human source for answers when something goes wrong in our lives. Meanwhile the LORD is waiting for us to simply ask

HIM! Believe that He who began a good work in you will bring it to completion.

The people that the LORD will use for our advancement may not be our initial choice because we view the world from a physical perspective while God looks at the heart. Thus someone may be brought into our lives for a short season, to usher us through a certain door where they hold the key to our entry. When their assignment is over that person is removed from our lives. A new season has been birthed in our lives.

Every new assignment comes with new responsibilities and accountability tied in. This is why we go through a time of hard testing before we're ushered into a spiritual promotion. The tools we've been using in our past job description will no longer work in our new assignment. Our new assignment requires a repositioning and restructuring of our minds, our relationships and strategies, often times extending to our emotional, spiritual and yes, sometimes even our physical spaces.

# Part 2: Learning the Faith Walk

# Chapter 5: The Power of Waiting in Faith

Now faith is the substance of things hoped for, the evidence of things not seen. Hebrews 11: 1 (KJV)

Faith has a voice: it's yours and it's mine. We each have to learn to exercise our faith voices in order to ignite the change that is necessary when we are being realigned for the new season in our journey of life.

In this section I share some faith-centred experiences that have helped to shape my life and the lives of others in the various communities I've been a part of.

The start of the above verse is inclusive: '**Now**' implies that we need to be continually employing faith in our daily walk and decision making. Speaking forth something that is not yet in existence will empower it to come into physical existence. Try it today by speaking forth your hopes and dreams and begin to create your reality.

How patient are you in waiting for your breakthrough? Just as a child learns to walk many months after birth, the manifestation of a promised reward may often take many seasons. We are now living in a microwave society where we all want our goodies now. If our miracle or gift doesn't materialise when we ask for it we start to behave like a spoilt child who can't accept the waiting process that is sometimes necessary before they receive their promised toy.

Interestingly, this trait did not begin with our generation. Look back over history and you will find that waiting is one of the most difficult things to do. However, when we wait for what we truly want and desire, we learn to appreciate that gift much more than if we received it instantaneously.

There are times when we speak forth what we've dreamt or witnessed in the spirit about something great that is about to happen to or for us. Be mindful that when you speak your dreams and visions you are not disempowering them or pushing them back a few years by proclaiming them in the wrong circles. Why? Because there are people who'd love for you to fail. What they put out into the atmosphere can delay your breakthrough through their unbelief, negative words and actions. Remember, the prophetic gifts and dreams that you have been given are not necessarily your friends, family members or other person's gifts. There is an individual path for each one of us to take. This path is in direct alignment with the divine purpose for which we each showed up in this world.

A prime example of this truth is found in the first Book of the Bible in Genesis 37 which records the events that followed 'Joseph the dreamer'. Joseph dreamt that the stars were bowing down to him, signifying that he would rule over his brothers and parents. Joseph was just a young lad when he had this dream. As the youngest member of the family,

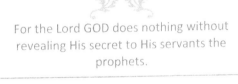

For the Lord GOD does nothing without revealing His secret to His servants the prophets.

Amos 3:7 (ESVUK)

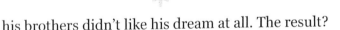

his brothers didn't like his dream at all. The result?

They threw Joseph in a pit, and later sold him as a slave. Joseph's fate was shifted from that point on. He spent many years serving as a slave for a crime he didn't commit. He was punished by Potipher's jealous wife for acting honourably. Joseph's two-year stint in prison taught him the importance of relying on the voice of God for wisdom, strength to endure, and especially humility. It was while in the prison dungeon that Joseph's gift of prophecy was sharpened, fuelled by humility and honesty. In the LORD's time Joseph ended up ruling over Egypt as second in command, answerable only to Pharaoh.

Did Joseph's dream come to pass? Yes. But the detour may have been avoided had Joseph learnt how to wait patiently, and not trust his siblings with every secret that was being revealed to him at such a young age.

Let's look at another example...

The prophet Jeremiah experienced the awesome nature of God as the LORD would often speak to him and then confirm His Word by bringing what was promised to pass shortly after. On one such occasion Jeremiah was imprisoned in the King's court for prophesying against the King of Judah. While he was incarcerated Jeremiah enquired of the LORD concerning the events that were about to take place. The LORD's response to Jeremiah:

I am the LORD, the God of all mankind. Is anything too hard for me? (Jeremiah 32:27, NIV)

The Bible records in Amos 3:7 that God does not do anything without first revealing it to His servants the prophets.

How will you know if a message spoken over you is from God? By the fruit it bears. If the prophecy comes to pass then it was from the Almighty. And if not?

There are numerous times when a prophecy does not manifest immediately. The physical manifestation may take days, weeks, months, years or even decades before the fruit of the word released germinates. This however does not mean that the word spoken over your life was false. Even though the vision tarries, WAIT FOR IT. Keep this in mind: 'Delayed is not denied'.

## Releasing Prophetic Faith
My earliest memory of prophetic words being spoken

> Wait patiently for the LORD. Be brave and courageous. Yes, wait patiently for the LORD.
>
> Psalm 27:14 (NLT)

over my life is over three decades ago. Yet some of these prophecies are only being manifested as I write this book! Delayed is not denied, my friend. Believe, expect and work towards the vision to activate it. Most importantly, have the faith and persistence that will shift your mountain to where it was instructed to move all those years ago!

You need to keep your eyes focused on your goal and vision. When I went through all the trying moments in my life that have changed the trajectory of my life, I often wondered if all that was spoken over me was just hot air blowing my way. I knew I could trust the LORD to come through, based on His track record of lifting me out of countless difficult situations. Nonetheless, my logical mind would often seek to sabotage my faith in the things unseen, yet promised to me. My mind sought to protect my ego just in case things didn't work out as the LORD had promised.

Has this ever happened to you? Have you been wondering when that wonderful moment of your breakthrough was going to walk into your life? Perhaps you've been waiting for the bell to chime to warn you that it was time to rise up to collect on that promise?

The more immediate questions to ponder are:

What steps have you taken towards walking into your God-promised destiny?

Have you started activating your faith through even the smallest action on your part, or have you been waiting for everything in your life to line up perfectly before you start taking action?

I ask because for a while all I saw in my life was a deep darkness which engulfed me, adding fear and a sense of desolation and hopelessness to the mix.

Clearly, I have since learnt that light and darkness never mix. The two are opposites that cannot cohabit the same space together. When light enters, darkness must depart.

To quote the words of a favourite song, I am also learning:

When darkness seems to veil His face, I rest on His unchanging grace. In every high and stormy gale, My anchor holds within the veil. On Christ, the Solid Rock I stand, All other ground is sinking sand. All other ground is sinking sand. [1]

(Lyrics by Edward Mote (1797-1874); Music by William Batchelder Bradbury (1816-1868))

Even though your prophecy tarries, wait, yes, wait patiently for it; for it will surely come to pass at the appointed time. Also, remain expectant and in faith for your vision to come to pass.

## The LORD Our Protector

I will lift my eyes toward the mountains. Where will my help come from? My help comes from the LORD, the Maker of heaven and earth. He will not allow your foot to slip; your Protector will not slumber. Psalm 121:1-3 (CSB)

I invite you to make the following words your own. As you claim them you will be strengthened from within. That's the secret place where no one can see or enter because they don't hold the key to your heart. But there is ONE who holds the key, and you can trust him to shift every negative thing from your life and restore your brokenness. He will give beauty for ashes, joy and restore a new song in your spirit. Read the following paragraph out loud and let them resonate within you. Even if you don't believe these words right now due to some storm you may be going through, take to re-reading and speaking them out daily and you will be amazed at the shift and inner peace that will begin to replace the sense of hopelessness and fear that had gripped you.

The LORD is my Protector. Indeed, He who watches over Israel never slumbers nor sleeps! He is my Rock, my Shield, my Strength and buckler, my Hiding Place, my Deliverer and my Peace through every storm I face in this life. My life is more precious to the LORD than I ever realised before going through the gruelling trials and moments of deep testing. As King David wrote, 'If the LORD had not been on my side...'

Are you feeling like you don't quite believe these words right now due to some storm you may be going through? That's ok. Just take a minute to read them aloud daily for 30 days and you will be amazed at the mental shift and inner peace that will begin to replace the sense of hopelessness and fear that had gripped you. This is a strategy that continues to work for me. Everything I share in this book is based on personal experience. Some do daily meditation. I choose to meditate on the promises of God who gave me life and breath.

## Be Fully Poured Out

We recently attended a 'maombolezi', which is a meeting to encourage and pray with a family who've lost a loved one. Within the Kenyan community in the UK we believe in activating the term 'iron sharpens iron'. Thus when a fellow sister or brother is in need, we pull together as a community and lend a hand to help meet the urgency – be it bereavement, illness, or other challenge.

My family lives in Birmingham where we hold monthly meetings to thank God for sustaining us and blessing the work of our hands. The members get to exhort one another with words of encouragement, often blessing the group in song, poetry, Scripture, dance or whatever other gifts the individuals have at their disposal. A speaker is also invited to share the Word for spiritual nourishment. Food and drink are often in plenty to nourish the physical body. I believe our parents taught us well: 'Bring what you have and let's all share – come one, come all.'

And so it was that my family went to console a dear family who recently lost their mother. I hear all the time how mothers are irreplaceable. This dear departed mother/grandma left behind a powerful legacy: in addition to impacting her immediate household, her life also touched her grandchildren, the taxi driver who often transported her to her hospital appointments, her carer and the hospital staff.

This ninety-something year old 'Cucu' (grandmother) had poured out her entire life into her community by selflessly sharing her wisdom. For instance, while her children were still in secondary school, this wise lady taught them how to invest by putting aside something little on a regular basis. When the grandchildren came along, she extended this wisdom to them too. She had birthed 14 children. Our friend was the youngest child. Our friend shared how every one of the siblings – and their working offspring – had learned and started applying these canny investment strategies as the LORD blessed the work of their hands.

I began to wonder: within the audience, was there a single other family that could honestly say they had been nurtured so powerfully by their parents or grandparents, as a community?

I was reminded that we each have a duty to impart whatever gift we've been blessed with to our children and to the upcoming generations down the line. Otherwise we would have fallen short of the commission we have been given in Proverbs 22:8 (NLT): 'Direct your children onto the right path, and when they are older, they will not leave it.' As adults then, it is our job to instruct our offspring along the path that leads to life. This is more important where youngsters do not have good or ideal role models surrounding them. In such a case, the youngsters may end up getting into trouble from being misled by selfish uncaring or misinformed folk who they hang around.

However, a 'well-watered' child from a tender age is much more likely to grow into a beautiful, well admired 'flower' that stands out in the crowd and brings honour and recognition to the 'nurturer' – the parent(s). 'Watering' our children with kindness, wise words and investing our time by sharing lifelong lessons will yield a bountiful harvest that others can glean from in due course.

Prayer:

May timely divine doors of favour open up to us to usher in our unique gifts and talents; may these open doors make room for us to shine in our world as we graciously pour ourselves out to others.

May we discover and freely choose to use our gifts and talents to serve others and make this world a better place because we passed by.

May we bring honour to our earthly parents and bestow honour, thanksgiving and praise to our heavenly Father for favouring us with such immeasurable gifts!

May you and I be fully poured out when our time comes to meet our Maker. May nothing of value be left within us when we depart this earth. In Jesus' Matchless Name! Amen.

# Chapter 6: Dealing with Injustice and Ill Health

What I learned through the confusing season of my life experience shared in the previous chapters is that bad things do not come to stay. It is important to put things into perspective. When the family I was once married into was abusing me and my family members they were simply doing what satisfied their ego. They experienced moments of power over us through their repeated taunting and intimidation.

Unfortunately, since we did not openly react or retaliate, they thought we were weak and therefore worth being demeaned further. And so they proceeded to pour more fuel to their fire. About ten months after I was widowed my former in-laws took me to court with the intent to disinherit my son. They made up some lies claiming I was not really married to their son. Yet I had an authentic certificate from Sheria House in Nairobi to prove that my marriage was legitimate. Their claims were ridiculous since some of their family had attended our marriage ceremony (my family didn't, but that's another story).

To then take me to court after emptying my home repeatedly and trying twice to physically steal my son was simply outrageous in every sense of the word. My baby was born four months after my husband died. So even while I was facing the trauma of bringing a child into the world without a husband to support me through this process (would have been nice I thought), I also had to contend with false accusations, theft of personal and household effects, cruelty and hostility to my staff, parents and siblings.

Marring into a different religion compounded matters. By God's grace the court case which lasted 5 and-a-half years ruled in my favour to keep my son and his inheritance. I gave my former in-laws a third of the inheritance to help complete the house we'd been building while my husband was alive. I just needed them to leave me alone. Thank God who always comes through for His children!

Admittedly my situation was the result of some bad choices I'd made, fuelled by a gross injustice. This plight led to 'survival of the fittest' mode, taking on three teaching jobs just to get by, performing and training more students to keep my mind off my troubles. The 'fight or flight mode' and 'workaholic' status during that season of my life were my coping strategies for the depression that followed; being seen to be vulnerable was not considered cool in my mind.

Shortly after the court case started I sought medical help to alleviate the distress and trauma going on. What started out as a visit to my GP led to my being referred to two more medical specialists: an endocrinologist and gynaecologist as there were all sorts of strange things going on with me. The cocktail of drugs the specialists prescribed were enough to knock me out a few times.

On one occasion I even fainted in my car at the Globe roundabout on my way to work. That's when I sought further medical attention, returning to my gynaecologist and explaining my symptoms and the after effects I was experiencing from the drug concoction. When the gynaecologist examined the packs he was shocked to learn that the tablets I'd been prescribed by the various specialists were all working against each other. Meaning that while one set of drugs was set to alleviate one type of problem or symptom, the other drugs acted as a propeller to magnify and heighten another medical issue, thereby playing havoc on both my body and mind. No wonder I was feeling light headed and hallucinating nearly every day!

The gynaecologist sought to change the drugs, but I had different plans in mind. Being fed up of what I was having to cope with on a daily basis, I simply informed him that was the last day I was going to take any of those drugs. He warned me of the doom and gloom scenario I was to expect from such drastic action: the likelihood of severe withdrawal symptoms from suddenly removing the entire cocktail from my daily dose. My response: 'What can be worse than what I'm going through right now, Doctor?' To which he responded after a thoughtful silence: 'See you in two weeks.' To the doctor's surprise and amazement when I returned to his surgery at our next appointment I was already looking and feeling better.

Being a man of faith, he said he'd been praying for

> Guard your heart above all else, for it determines the course of your life.
> Proverbs 4:23 (NLT)

me. I was thankful to hear that as myself and others had been praying for my healing too.

It was shortly after that I sought a scholarship to further my studies abroad, as a way to make a fresh start and get my PhD at the same time. This was the turning point I needed, the cool breeze that kept me from packing it all in.

Through all this, I learnt that alone I can do nothing. With God however, all things are possible. This truth was so liberating and empowering. Today I firmly believe that nothing will happen to me today that my God cannot take care of. As I invite the LORD into my daily life, I trust that He will lead and guide my footsteps and keep me grounded and focused. I choose to keep a continuous connection with the Holy Spirit, for all of my help comes from the LORD!

Surely there is a place of quiet rest and peace... near to the heart of God.

I pray you will find that place every day as you commit your days to Him.

## Guarding Your Heart: A Life Lesson

Isn't it wonderfully releasing that everything we need for life and good health is found in the Scriptures! If we are wise, we will follow the instructions found in the Bible. This Good Book will guide our path and lead us in green pastures as Psalm 23 reminds us.

Yet the older we grow it seems the less we tend to listen or even seek out this wise instruction. What a folly! The foolish mistakes I have made in my tender life have served to illuminate the truth that I am not capable of leading an excellent or even an admirable life on my own strength. I realise that I need a Helper who will constantly seek to steer my ship towards the right direction whenever I find myself going off course.

This is sometimes an inconvenience since in my carnal thinking there are numerous distractions that tend to look quite appealing as an alternative route to where I'm headed. I wonder if you too have on occasion made a decision that seemed easier, faster, and more comfortable, all based on your own thinking or 'head knowledge'? I know I have. How did that go for you? In my case not very well. I ended up getting my fingers – and sometimes much more – burnt. Thank God for the opportunity to take a right turn and let go of the rudder that steers my ship, and allow the Holy Spirit to guide my path!

When it comes to matters of the heart, taking a wrong turn can be very costly, sometimes to the extent of ensuing death. Sadly, this is what happened

---

Do not expose your heart to negative influences or you will face some painful consequences. Dr Jackie Samuels

---

in my case.

Was it instinct that caused Mom to warn me to stay clear of a wrong choice? It was much more, namely the Holy Spirit guiding me through someone valuable in my life - Mom. Yet for some unknown reason I chose (foolishly) to ignore her warning. Oh what a senseless and unnecessary thing! See the folly of immature stubbornness coupled with being pushed over the edge.

**A word of caution for parents:** Be careful where you make your life altering plans, dear parents! Please, please do not try to plan every minute detail of your children's lives, lest you send them to the deep abyss!

I recall once asking Mom what she thought I should do in a certain situation. When she asked me what my choices were, i recounted the three choices. To my surprise Mom then told me to go with my gut instinct. When I tried pressing Mom to discover what choice she would have made in my situation, she responded that now that I was an adult I needed to learn to make my own decisions. After pondering her response, I came to the conclusion that when I make a mistake I should take the responsibility for it and then seek to rectify it if it goes pear shaped. That was a wake-up call to adulthood and independence.

As adults we are constantly faced with serious decisions to make. Trouble comes when we choose to always look outside of ourselves for the answers. I'm learning in my current family that being a wife, mother and entrepreneur is not the easiest thing in the world. There are choices I have to make that affect others. On the flip side, when I'm guiding others I'm careful not to force a solution upon them. That responsibility lies squarely with them to make. The greatest thing I've found in all this is that we have One greater than us to whom we can always turn with expectant hearts and the full assurance that He will provide us with the correct answers for every situation. He never fails us.

Never give up on doing what you believe to be right. If in doubt, ask for divine intervention through prayer and meditation. Above all, always remain steadfast to your calling. Remember to always diligently and consciously guard your heart. Here's why...

You reap what you sow.

Sow in tears, reap in joy; sow in anger, reap confusion and contention; sow in bitterness, reap sour grapes... you get the picture. Psalm 126:5 (NIV) states: *Those who sow with tears will reap with songs of joy.*

Suffice it to say that I sowed many tears in the short time I was married to this man. We all fall down at some point in life. Thankfully change comes when we choose to get up again. Having repented for my error in judgment and disobedience to my parents, I now take the time to counsel youngsters who are considering taking that unsafe forest road, when they ask for my advice. Ultimately, the choice remains theirs to make.

# Chapter 7: Speaking and Doing

> God is not human that He should lie,
> not a human being, that He should
> change His mind. Does He speak and
> then not act? Does He promise and not
> fulfil?
>
> Numbers 23:19 (NIVUK)

We ought to utilise these wonderful power Scriptures as we daily step out in faith by employing the power of the spoken word. When your spirit is disquieted within you, use the Word to get back into alignment and increase your faith. Remember that when God Speaks, He Does What He Says He Will Do.

There is a wonderful principle at work here. The LORD God Almighty is a Promise Keeper. He is not a man to lie or change His mind, or the son of man to repent. Meaning, you and I can always rely on the WORD from the LORD. This amazing promise reminds me of the hymn: '*We have an anchor that keeps the soul, steadfast and sure while the billows roll. Fastened to the Rock which cannot move, grounded firm and deep in the Saviour's love.'*

This truly is Love Divine. Is there a song humming softly within your spirit when things are going wrong? What strength can you draw on in times of deep testing?

My spirit often tunes in to the chorus of the above lyrics. My comfort comes from an inner knowledge that a bigger force within me knows all about my challenges. Because He is concerned He's constantly reminding me of His Presence and ultimate will to deliver me from the chains that would often seek to cloud my mind and render me powerless to break free from.

In time I have also come to understand that my present situation is not here to stay, it will pass in time.

If you find yourself taking a wrong turn and someone you trust and respect warns you to stop, it may well be your saving grace if you choose to listen to their wise counsel. Learn to trust a wise adult's instinct. Tune in and listen, carefully consider their advice, and more importantly, take appropriate action in order to save yourself possible years of misery later on. You will find that they have been blessed with a special wisdom when dealing with spiritual matters. Here are some points to ponder as you move into your new season:

What is the LORD saying to you? How is His Word being rooted within your spirit? Where is He leading you? Who is He aligning your path with to walk alongside you? Who are your Destiny Helpers?

Finding the responses to these questions will help you get clear on how to align with your vision, direction and the timing of God for your life in the next chapter of your precious life. Back to the most trusted Word:

We have a wonderful promise relayed by the Prophet Isaiah in the Book of Isaiah 55:10-12 (NIVUK):

As the rain and the snow come down from heaven, and do not return to it without watering the earth and making it bud and flourish, so that it yields seed for the sower and bread for the eater, so is My Word that goes out from My mouth: it will not return to Me empty, but will accomplish what I desire and achieve the purpose for which I sent it. You will go out in joy and be led forth in peace; the mountains and hills will burst into song before you, and all the trees of the field will clap their hands.

When the LORD speaks to us and about us, He ALWAYS performs His Word. That is His faithful action-centred character! Hallelujah!

When we as God's beloved children choose to trust Him implicitly, His all-surpassing peace will guard our hearts and our minds in Christ Jesus, as Philippians 4:7 reminds us. When distractions threaten to persuade us to put the LORD aside, remember when we call Him He will answer us.

## The Power of Decisiveness: Learning to Say 'No'

Do you know how many people fall victim to the fear of saying 'No'? They end up saying 'Yes' out of fear of possible unpleasant repercussions, or to avoid having to explain why they said 'No'. I have learned from following wise leaders that it is indeed safe to say 'No'.

For instance, Steve Jobs attributes his success with Apple to his learning to say 'No'. He learnt the power of staying focused and true to his vision and following his dream.

When you learn to say 'No' you will sometimes find that is the most loving response. People will respect you for your honesty. It is much better to recognise how much you are able to be available for some folk than to promise to commit to a task, only to default later. Learn to harness nurturing relationships based on respect by exercising the power of 'No'.

This act will also release you from overwhelm and overburdening your days and life with inconsequential things that don't advance your life's purpose. Learning when to say 'No' will also make room for you to focus on the path that moves you closer to aligning with your divine calling and life purpose.

## Busy-ness or Rest?

Then, because so many people were coming and going that they did not even have a chance to eat, He said to them, "Come with me by yourselves to a quiet place and get some rest." Mark 6:31 (NIVUK)

The above Scripture refers to Master Jesus who was on a mission to teach His disciples how to live victorious lives. Here we see two nutritional elements to the process: spiritual and practical or physical. The disciples needed to balance their time between ministering to the crowds and physical rest. The rest was an essential part of their mission so that they would each receive the strength and instruction from the heavenly Father for the work that was to follow shortly thereafter.

The same principle applies to us. In this day and age where there are so many hindrances and good causes constantly seeking our undivided attention, we need to set aside some time to retune and recharge our physical, emotional and spiritual batteries. Otherwise if we run our batteries dry we will also run out of steam. Then we'll be no good to anyone, least of all ourselves. Our effectiveness as nurturers, encouragers, educators, healers, mentors, or whatever world transforming role each one plays in our sphere of influence, is directly linked to our taking care of the most important person: self. This is not being selfish, it is providing self-care. This is an important distinction, one that many tend to overlook because of incorrect teaching or interpretation.

Learning to be still is an art. It takes great courage and absolute obedience to stop being 'busy', running around like a headless chicken trying to be superwoman or superman and simply 'be'.

This has been one of the hardest things for me to learn to apply in my own life. If you ask my hubby Peter, he will tell you the number of times he finds me busy buzzing around even when I have been advised to rest.

Yet, amazingly, when I do choose to take time to rest

---

When we practice self-care by resting, we are recharging our physical, emotional and spiritual batteries.

---

and be still, that inner still small Voice I have come to know and love so well will always reach out to me. The Holy Spirit has a special way of ensuring He gets my attention so that He can instruct me. Sometimes that sweet Voice confirms something that I have been mulling over for a while, not knowing quite who to ask or what to do about it.

In my second phase of married life, I am grateful for many things. During my (decade + and counting) wonderful marriage to Peter, I have come to recognise that when we are discussing a serious issue, that discussion is a form of prayer since we often end many discussions with prayer. So next time you are sharing something that is close to your heart with someone you love, trust and who shares the same belief as you, remember there is One who's right there in your midst. When you commit the discussion and entrust the outcome to Him, be sure to only expect the very best outcome possible. This promise is available to all God's children.

Remember, He stands at the door and knocks, awaiting a welcome into our conversations and life decisions. When we usher Him in, He takes over and supplies the answers we seek.

The Holy Spirit is a 'Gentleman' who will never force His way or gate-crash into your life; He'll always wait to be welcomed in.

When you do, you'll be grateful for the positive input into your life. Try it today and experience this loving life change for yourself.

Take time to listen to the Father's Voice and seek His perfect will. Jesus Christ constantly withdrew to a quiet place to pray and renew His spirit and inner strength. The miracles that followed these frequent times of stillness were always profound, as recorded in the Gospels. God's plans for you and me are always for our good, to give us a hope and future. As we wait patiently for the LORD He will incline His ear to us. That's a principle with an unfailing promise, well worth embracing.

## Stillness and Listening

In stillness we hear the quiet inner voice that speaks to us in a gentle voice. And then it's our job to take good, orderly direction from God. Remember the verse and song: 'Be still and know that I am God'? The song's melody is contemplative, gentle and peaceful with a slow tempo. The character of the melody complements the words of the Psalmist:

"*Be still, and know that I am God; I will be exalted among the nations, I will be exalted in the earth.*" Psalm 46: 10; (ESV)

Russell Simmons, a great entrepreneur used to think that anxiety and insomnia were his drivers to success. Then he realised that it was the stillness that enabled him be good at anything.

Gabrielle Bernstein is the author of 'Miracles Now: 108 Life-Changing Tools for less stress, more flow & finding your true purpose'. Gabrielle states:

'When you extend the seconds of stillness, that's when you're able to think and learn. Living a guided life is about extending the seconds of stillness. As we add up the moments of stillness we feel life begin to flow. What we need comes directly to us. Life lessons are no longer difficult. We have a greater awareness of our purpose and connection to the world. Stillness is where it's at'. I concur.

## Decision Making and Timing

Too often we feel pressured by the number of things that need to get done at any point in the day. It is particularly at these times that we would benefit from stopping, taking a step back and focussing on being still. Even a moment of stillness can change one's destiny from making irrational decisions based on the pressure and stress of the moment. The amazing Greek-American author Ariana Huffington, who is also co-founder and Editor-in-chief of the Huffington Post says, '*Never make a decision when you are hungry, tired, angry or lonely*'. There is great wisdom in Ariana's words of warning.

Here's a timely quote by Ariana, mother of two daughters:

'Fearlessness is like a muscle. I know from my own life that the more I exercise it the more natural it becomes to not let my fears run me. But you have to do what you dream of doing even while you're afraid. I think while all mothers deal with feelings of guilt, working mothers are plagued by guilt on steroids!'

Take a moment and look back to some regretful decisions you may have made in the past. Were any of those unfortunate decisions made when you were in a state of anger, hunger, tiredness or loneliness? Let's add to the list stress and feeling pressured by someone to say 'yes' instantly, particularly when the magnitude of the request or situation called for unpressured and considered thought and clarity before committing to accepting to take on the task.

It's time to take stock and make the necessary amendments if you want to change your decision-making pattern. Learn to operate from a position of strength by only making definitive decisions when you are fresh, alert, present in the moment and after according yourself sufficient thinking time when necessary. This may well save you many costly years of agony, pain and financial loss in the long run.

I am grateful for my family and the caring neighbours who looked out for us during a time of uncertainty and turmoil, and especially for my younger brother Isaac who came to live with me. This was necessary for many reasons. Having a man around the home was essential, providing us with respected male protection. It also acted as a deterrent to my oppressors: the knowledge that there was someone of authority – a tall male no less - who they'd have had to answer to if they'd continued their attacks on us.

Understanding the psychology of these former in-laws is important because I had been in a cross-cultural marriage where that community looked down on women. Since I didn't realise the extent of this misguided mindset at the time, it came as a great shock be subjected to physical and emotional abuse. Having grown up thinking that most people were generally kind, I had also witnessed my parents fighting on a few occasions. Some of our neighbours' wives were also terrorised by their husbands, as we could hear the commotion through the open windows. Despite these episodes happening around me, to learn that this could happen to me as well was horrifying. What do they say about girls being attracted to men that look or behave like their dads? Let me assure you that this was farthest from my mind.

During the long court case the agonising loneliness nearly caused me to give up hoping for a better life. I'm now grateful for the grace to push through, making me deeply appreciate the phrase, *'This too shall pass'*.

Whenever I find myself getting overwhelmed by the cares of this world, I tune in within to the music of my soul. There are times in life when it becomes virtually impossible to articulate the level of deep pain and agonies tormenting the spirit within.

Yet during these darkest moments my peace comes from deep inner worship. By infilling my spirit with praise and comforting words that speak life into the situation, my spirit is restored, refreshed and revived. Then eventually the voice comes into alignment with the inner worship going on within and the audible sound bursts forth. Yes indeed, 'praise will confuse the enemy', as Pastor Marvin Sapp declares through his powerfully uplifting song.

Let's focus on you for a moment:

***Have you been experiencing tormenting moments of confusion and distress?*** Are you trying to make sense of it all? It's alright to cry. It's okay to be still, to be quiet and in that reflective mood you will begin to feel a beautiful calmness engulf you and a sense of inner peace embracing you from within. Don't try to explain every emotion you are going through. I have found that my most painful and emotionally cutting experiences have somehow made me stronger and more resilient to what life throws my way. My restoration has been an ongoing journey as I surrender to the healing process.

What keeps me is my faith in the One True Living God who lives in me and loves me. The Almighty already knew I would have to endure such agony. He also provided strategic helpers throughout my journey; each one has played their part in restoring hope and a semblance of normalcy to my life – yes, this is important. Even now the LORD provides people who speak life into my spirit and into whatever situation that comes my way. The same provision is available to you my friend.

Heartache left unchecked leads to all sorts of illness and dis-ease. Illness is your body's way of telling you it needs a helping hand. Whether it's depression, insomnia, blood pressure, fear, agoraphobia or any other ailment, nothing should keep you hidden behind locked doors, away from the world, for fear of being crushed by the people you used to love being around. Are you presently tiptoeing through life because you are afraid to offend someone, fearing the repercussions of honestly expressing your opinion?

Remember you're not the first or the last to go through such feelings; I've too been there. If you find your mind threatening to regress to unhealthy reactions when faced with situations that remind you of past traumas you'll need to address your fears head-on, otherwise they will continue to derail your God-given future. 2 Timothy 1:7 reminds us:

'For God has not given us a spirit of fear, but of power and of love and of a sound mind.' (NKJV)

Understand that the world is not against you, they just do not understand your pain. They have not walked the same path as you. Your reactions may be foreign to your family, your friends, colleagues, even your neighbours. When you need a helping hand, ask the LORD for help.

**Declaration**: My help comes from the LORD, the Maker of the heavens and the earth. He will not let my foot stumble. The LORD watches over me, to perfect what He has started in me.

My husband Peter has a special saying he heard from another pastor, which I'll pass on to you:

'Faith has a voice: It's MINE. God has a people: It's ME. The devil can try his best, but his best is not good enough.'

---

Whenever I find myself getting overwhelmed with the cares of this world, I tune in to the music of my soul.

---

It's time to use your faith voice, precious one.

**Action**:

What's one way you will use your faith voice to declare positive change in your life today?

# Chapter 8: The Message of Hope

---

'Call to me and I will answer you and tell you great and unsearchable things you do not know.'

Jeremiah 33:3 (NIV)

---

Christ Jesus is touched by the feeling of our infirmity. When Jesus came and lived among us, He wanted to experience what we experience. He wanted to come to our level so that we could connect with Him on an even keel. So instead of Christ appearing to us as being so high and mighty and living somewhere up in the clouds, Christ came down to earth and lived as one with us. One of the names of Christ Jesus is 'Emmanuel', meaning 'God with us'. This is why He is able to reach out to us and we can take His hand, hear His voice, and know His heart's desire for us. He feels our pain, hears our heart's cry, holds our hands and hearts, and leads us out of the miry clay and into the safety of His protection. Christ Jesus is able to set our feet upon the Rock – that is Himself.

What a great message! The message of hope is available to every one of us on this earth. Hope that things will get better in our lives. Hope that the mess we've made can be turned into something of beauty and value, that we can indeed bring honour to our Creator, despite our ugly start in life. Only God could deck the cards in our favour, and wipe our slate clean! What a wonderful truth to embrace with confidence and gratitude!

If you've been hurt and betrayed by someone you loved and trusted, and are ready to change the direction of your life moving forward, you need to release all the pain of being let down. You need to forgive others who have hurt you. If you don't forgive others who have wronged you, how will you be able to move on? Forgive them and release yourself from the agony of carrying this burden that you don't have to carry. It's time to lay your burden down.

Most of all, you need to forgive yourself. This is KEY.

Forgive yourself for feeling so unworthy. Forgive yourself for lacking the faith to trust or believe again. Forgive yourself for believing the lies going on in your head. Forgive yourself for believing and internalising the lies of the enemy broadcast through other people and your own self-doubt. Once you forgive the past, with all its lies, it's time to embrace your truth. You are creating your new reality, your truth. Embrace the following truths:

You are awesome. You are one of a kind. You are appreciated. You are loved.

You are unique. The gifts you possess no one else has. You are stronger than you think you are.

The seeds of greatness are already within you.

You were brought into this world to make a difference with your special gifts.

Perhaps right now you feel like there's no strength left in you to reclaim your power and worth. You may be feeling as if someone has burst the balloon in your tummy and 'winded you out of service' - at least for the moment. And that's okay.

I have good news for you. Take time to love yourself back to health, back to feeling worthy, feeling valued and valuable, back to feeling awesome. Make no apology for the time it will take you to get back on track. Remember, all the misfortunes and negative experiences you've gone through have taken time. Therefore, you will need to make the shift and start to embrace your healing and newness using 'time' as your friend.

I'm speaking from the heart here because this is exactly what I have had to do to get back in the game of believing in myself, and believing that I was created to accomplish greater things than feeling sorry for myself because of all the misfortunes life has dealt me.

Here's a beautiful quote that ignites me: 'If at first you try and don't succeed, try, try, try again'. [William Edward Hickson]

How about that? Change takes time. Time is a great shifter of perspective and rewarder of courage. Every time you choose to forgive a wrong, an offense, an undesirable action, you free yourself from the

---

The message of hope is available to every person on earth. Hope that things will get better in your life. Hope activates Faith.

---

bondage of self-limiting your effectiveness and enjoyment of the life you've been accorded.

## Embrace the Power of Making Right Choices

Your life is a GIFT. Choose today to embrace the gift that resides in YOU. I encourage you to speak mindfully to your inner self:

> ➢ I am awesomely and wonderfully unique.

- I have greatness within me. I am thankful for my life today.

- My God will supply all my needs according to His glorious riches.

- Nothing about this day will take God by surprise so I choose to trust my God because He will take care of my day in every way.

- I choose to align myself with my Higher Power who will do immeasurably, abundantly, above and beyond all I can ever ask, think, or hope for. This is my heritage as a child of the living God.

- There is something great for me in this day and I choose to show up for it today. Today I choose Faith over fear.

- Today I choose to let go of all doubt, fear, feelings of helplessness and hopelessness, unforgiveness and bitterness.

- Today I choose to let go of all negative thoughts and actions that have been derailing my progress.

- Today I choose to align myself with positive minded people who uplift me and accept me for who I am.

- I am open to learning new ways of being awesome and sharing awesomeness with others today.

➤ I choose to show up with a positive spirit for the miracles awaiting me today. I choose to share kindness, joy, love and hope with others and myself today.

➤ I choose Love. I choose Joy. I choose Peace. I choose Faith. I choose Favour. I choose Boldness.

➤ I choose to show gratitude in the little things that happen to me today. This gratitude will expand into the big things in my life and around me.

---

Remember that change takes time. Purpose today to make the vital shift needed in your life. Start to embrace your healing and newness using time as your friend.

Dr Jackie Samuels

---

Key Takeaway: What you focus on expands.

Choose to focus on positive thoughts, positive emotions, positive actions, positive interactions, positive music, positive books, positive news and media, positive conversations, positive awareness, positive acts of kindness and positive declarations.

As your positive actions expand with your conscious activation, watch as your positive reality starts to unfold daily in your life.

"Yesterday is history...Tomorrow is a mystery...Today is a gift...That's why it's called the present!" - Author unknown Choose to live your life in the Gift of Today. Point to ponder: How are you embracing change in your life?

# Chapter 9: Creativity and Doing Good

> Most people have no idea of the giant capacity we can immediately command when we focus all of our resources on mastering a single area of our lives. - Anthony Robbins

Creating mastery in one area of our lives is what will get us to be noticed. We will become the 'go to' person who others are seeking for advice, help and direction. We will be seen as the authority in that one area.

Isn't it better to become a master of one area or discipline that others struggle with and need our services, than to simply be a 'Jack of all trades' that no one ever looks up to for advice and direction?

What is your passion?

Where is your creative strength?

What comes naturally to you?

In what areas do you find your creative juices flowing most frequently and effortlessly?

When you wake up each morning, what is your first 'aha' moment thought that sets your creative explorative mind on fire?

Perhaps the answer is found in your dreams and desires: What do you dream about in those quiet moments of stillness, when you allow your mind to wander off into the sunset?

We each discover our 'aha' moments through different experiential avenues. It's not always possible to use someone else's 'aha' trigger to seek to trigger your own passion point or to pinpoint your chief areas of strength.

It may also be the case that you are blessed with more than one area of strength, and that's great. You can use all your strengths to shape your future moving forward.

Align yourself with what you do best, that is what comes naturally for you which may also be what others struggle with. Use your creative gifts to do good to others, with others and for others. Your creative talents and skills are a gift from the Giver of all good gifts, our heavenly Father. He has blessed each and every one of us with something that we can bring to the table in order to empower another soul, thus sharing love through our serving and empowering others.

James 1:17 (NLT) reminds us that Whatever is good and perfect comes down to us from God our Father, who created all the lights in the heavens. He never changes or casts a shifting shadow.

That's an awesome truth right there. All our gifts are good. They are sent to us by the heavenly Father of lights whose nature is goodness. Light is good. Light also dispels darkness. So as we live in the light, looking to the Light Giver, we become the light for someone else.

As we burst forth with our light, we dispel the darkness from another person's world, soul and life. Since our Light Source lives within us, empowering us, breathing newness and illuminating His light all around us, we too can show others the light. What a beautiful world we are creating when we share God's Light around the world! Our gifts are the light-source that others will see in and through us. Therefore, let's sharpen those skill-swords so that we are empowered and released to offer the best light possible to all who need to tap into our light. We therefore have a duty to become the best stewards of the light bestowed upon us.

Following is a wonderful Scripture that over the years has helped me gain some perspective about the reality of the changing (and sometimes painful) nature of the times and seasons in our precious lives:

Romans 8:16-18 (ESV)

*The Spirit himself bears witness with our spirit that we are children of God, and if children, then heirs—*

*heirs of God and fellow heirs with Christ, provided we suffer with Him in order that we may also be glorified with Him. For I consider that the sufferings of this present time are not worth comparing with the glory that is to be revealed to us.*

What does it mean '...to be glorified with Him', or as in other versions, '... to share in His glory'?

As children of God and joint heirs with Christ what we experience in this life will fade when we receive the glory being prepared for us as we journey through life, and when we meet the LORD.

Meanwhile, I am reminded that every single life experience we have will be used to benefit us and others in some way as we grow in wisdom and obedience, walking uprightly before GOD and our fellow brothers and sisters.

These truths uncovered the following:

A certainty that all my past sufferings have been a preparation for the LORD's favour and glory which is about to be bestowed upon me and my family.

The events I have shared in this book have been about a time of immense testing intended to sharpen my spiritual being as a child of God. The need to create a trusting relationship in my heavenly Father.

The knowledge that God will always lead me in green pastures and will lift me out of muddy waters.

At times there will be some 'loud' visible scars as evidence that I too passed through the mud and mire. However, I also know that He didn't bring me this far to leave me by the side of the road.

Jesus promises me, 'I will not leave you comfortless'. For as long as I shall live I will testify of the LORD's love, goodness, grace and mercy upon my life. Fellow Gospel singer-songwriter and actress Vicki Rohe sang the song 'Testify' whose words constantly minister to my soul.

There is a deep lesson to be learned from this chapter too: Walk in obedience to the LORD our Creator and reap the rewards of our faithfulness.

I know for certain that God is faithful. He is fair. He promises never to test us beyond what we can handle. When we feel weighed down by the trials we face, we have an anchor that keeps the soul steadfast and sure through life's changing seasons. Our God is faithful, compassionate, and a promise keeper.

As we live in the light, looking to the Light Giver, we become the light for someone else. As we burst forth with our light, we dispel the darkness from another person's world, soul and life.

## God's Goodness

God is good. He is my light and salvation. He never changes His loving, caring and good character. As a result, He alone remains trustworthy and true in every sense of the word.

As Psalm 85:12 (NIVUK) promises us:

*Indeed, the LORD will give what is good, and our land will yield its produce.*

I declare that your land will yield its produce from the good you have been blessed with. This means that you already have good birthed within you. You only need to tap into it, nurture the good within you, and use it to nurture, bless and empower others. We have been blessed to be a blessing. The favour bestowed on us is not designed to be hidden away or dismissed as being unimportant or inconsequential. Rather, our gifts are to be used to empower the wider community. We have a mission and unction to align with our Divine calling. We have a responsibility to apply our gifts in excellence, and to utilise them fully to nurture who we are becoming. As we grow we guide and empower others to excel in life by using our gifts, skills and talents.

The great leaders and most successful men and women among us have learned this secret. The successful folk I have had the pleasure and honour to study all have one thing in common: they have committed to sharpening their skills, then sharing their expertise with others, and by so doing empowering others. The remuneration that follows is an outcome of the teaching and nurturing process.

Please understand the order of events: First is discovering the gifts, second is sharpening of the gifts; thirdly sharing the gifts, lastly receiving (monetary and other) rewards for sharing those gifts or talents. Which leads us to the crucial question:

## How are You Sharpening Your Gifts?

Over the past decade I have committed to investing some of my earnings in personal development. You may have heard the phrase: '*A student is only as good as the teacher*'. If the teacher is not so skilled in their subject area, what happens to the students? Have you observed this happening around you? What effects does such a scenario have on the wider community?

In my teaching career I have come across a few mentors who are not up to scratch with their trade. I'm making no judgments here, it's only an observation. I propose that the remedy for this skill deficiency in such persons is to commit to investing in targeted personal development in the area of skill enhancement needed in order to sharpen their teaching and delivery skills. Only then will one be well able to pass on the skillset as required in the workplace.

Whether you are an entrepreneur, business owner, manager, departmental head, or anyone seeking to empower others - first empower yourself then use your skills to sharpen and effectively guide those you mentor.

There is room for the person who is willing to show themselves approved through continual self-growth.

For surely, your gifts will make room for you.

# Part 3: The Inner Healing Process

**A cheerful heart is good medicine, but a crushed spirit dries up the bones.**

Proverbs 17:22

# Chapter 10: Embracing Peace in Relationships

The Key to your success lies in releasing the past in order to embrace the present. While holding on to the past it's impossible to thrive in the present. Yet the present is what ushers you into the wonderful future that lies in store for you.

In this section we'll explore how recognising what was happening in my present as a result of choices made in the past was keeping me captive in a place I did not ask or wish to be. In order to do this, we first need to…

## Understand Cultural Backgrounds and Communication Differences

In my two decades of working with children and young people with special educational needs (SEN) in schools in the UK, I've been astounded by the deep understanding and empathy that exists within the SEN communities I've had the absolute honour to work in – essentially between the adults and youngsters. Working with young people with various learning disabilities has unfolded a new communication language in my world, a language that embraces both verbal and non-verbal communication.

Watching some of these youngsters go on to create their future in the wider world has revealed something precious within my spirit: that all the seeds of greatness the adults - parents, staff, social workers, carers, family members, etc. - have sown and watered in these youngsters have been well worth every investment of time, faith, love, belief, words of hope and encouragement. It may well have taken tons of patience, faith and perseverance in many instances, but the effort has been well worth it. When we do all things in love with patience, beautiful miracles begin to unfold right before our eyes.

I have learnt that there is a depth of love, wisdom and empathy deep within us that can only be tapped into though an innate, purposeful understanding of the language of communication that every individual operates in.

Have you ever been faced with a situation where you were in a new environment and could not seem to fathom the people's jokes, meaning of the phrases and words used to describe a situation, despite the fact that they were speaking a familiar language to you? How is it that you could not understand the meaning of their words relayed in a familiar tongue? Could it be that your cultural differences and communication styles clashed in this instance?

Verbal communication does not always fulfil the purpose of understanding the intricate depth of information hidden within us. Where verbal communication is limited, we can learn these hidden meanings and nuances by tapping into the various non-verbal communication channels available to us. It is important to recognise that every case is different. Every person is unique and requires an individual approach in order to successfully communicate one's true desires, feelings, wants and needs.

How does this knowledge and realisation relate to communicating with people within the home, between friends, and between people who have grown up in different communities? This is a deep subject that requires in-depth discussion to uncover the hidden meanings contained within certain covert actions and expressions between two people who meet for the first time, hailing from different cultural backgrounds, communicating different languages, and having different life experiences.

Imagine someone close to you gets into a relationship with a person from a different culture. Now imagine these two people speak different languages and have different religious beliefs and perhaps even grew up in different environments (e.g. city verses country). This scenario poses a myriad of potential challenges right at the outset. Each of the above challenges would require specific strategies and approaches to overcome successfully without totally damaging the two concerned individuals' world.

Notice also how each challenge described above represents the need for a new language of communication to be learned by the two individuals in order to minimise conflict further into their relationship. Moreover, the two families involved would do well to familiarise themselves with these communication channels in order to effectively provide appropriate counsel, direction and guidance to the individuals in love. All these systems would be essential to ensuring damage control in case of the relationship potentially going sour.

When the right communication languages are not in place, any later breakup in the relationship can have a devastating outcome. This would result in a lot of bewildered and deeply hurt people, left to pick up the pieces with little or no understanding of the root cause of the breakdown. Understanding the root cause of such a disturbing breakdown is the significant key to establishing damage control strategies geared towards helping manage the after effects of relationships that have broken down as a result of cultural, religious and other language barriers.

Realise also that failure to at least attempt to repair such damage can easily lead to long-term discouragement, feelings of failure and unworthiness, depression, and loss of faith in the power of true love.

2 Corinthians 6:14 warns us not to be unequally yoked with unbelievers. This scripture likens such union to light and darkness trying to dwell together. Eventually, one will overcome the other. Heeding this warning would help to avoid such pain and disappointment as described above.

## What's Love Got to Do with it?

This is a loaded question which I'll do my best to answer with scriptural guidance.

Love has everything to do with building strong lasting relationships that can be nurtured and honoured to withstand the test of time.

In 1 Corinthians chapter 13 we have been gifted the perfect 'love manual' for living in unity, respect, honour, and for sustaining hope, faith and perseverance in our relationships. Do you want to live a strong, healthy, happy, fruitful loving relationship with your fellow brothers and sisters, in your home, workplace and community? Do all things in love.

## First, What Love Is Not...

Let's break down some of the nuggets shared in this well-loved Scripture.

1 Corinthians 13:1 likens our speaking in all the languages of earth and of angels, without love for others, as being akin to a noisy gong or a clanging cymbal. Imagine whenever you spoke out for something you believed to be adding value to the discussion, being perceived as a noisy gong! Imagine constantly being ridiculed and put down, interrupted with a snide remark whenever you cared to share your opinion in the presence of others...

What would that do to your self-esteem, your confidence in sharing your valuable thoughts, or your relationships with others? How would that impact your mind and the way you viewed yourself and your world? What lasting damage might that result in for you and those closest and dearest to you? This should not happen. Sadly, there are people around us who seem to thrive in inflicting emotional pain and abuse upon others, perhaps as a way to make themselves feel more powerful and command fear from the victims. Wouldn't it be more profitable to be civil, respecting others and treating them the same way they would wish to be treated?

1 Corinthians 13:2-3 records that if we had various gifts and possessed all knowledge, had great faith but lacked love, we would be nothing. We might even give everything to the poor to the extent of sacrificing our bodies, and boast about our actions, but without love, all our giving and boasting amounts to nothing. If you happen to see someone showing off without displaying any empathy or concern for others, beware of their real motives and steer clear lest you become a victim of their big self-serving, harmful egos.

## Second, The Fragrance and Character of LOVE

There follows in verses 4-7 of 1 Corinthians 13 the profound definitions of the fragrance and character of love.

 (Verse 4 –5) Love is patient and kind. Love is not jealous or boastful or proud or rude. Love does not demand its own way. Love is not irritable, and it keeps no record of being wronged.

V6 – Love does not rejoice about injustice; instead, love rejoices whenever the truth wins out.

V7 – Love never gives up, never loses faith, is always hopeful and endures through every circumstance.

V8-10 describes the gifts that will fade away when the perfect comes, all the imperfect things will disappear, including prophecy, speaking in unknown tongues, and partial knowledge.

The crowning statement is found in the final verse of this powerful chapter (verse 13):

Three things will last forever – faith, hope and love – and the greatest of these is LOVE.

My realisation from this awesome passage:

1. It is impossible to love another person to the fullest extent possible while you are still hurting from the effects and breakdown of love and trust from a previous relationship.

2. Forgiveness is the key to unlocking the freedom and ability to fully love again, to be able to accept and embrace another's love as being genuine towards you.

3. Commit to releasing the past deceptions and disappointments of false love which turned out to be the other person abusing your sincerity and genuine love for their selfish ambitions and purposes.

4. Time is a great healer. Conversely, time can also be a great destroyer. The choice lies solely with you to either

a. Choose to remain unforgiving, continue blaming the other party for ruining your life by mistreating or thwarting you and not valuing your love, or embrace the higher path...

b. Choose to forgive someone who has wronged and hurt you deeply, even if they have toyed with your mind by discounting your precious gift of love towards them. This includes people who may have rejected your love, not understood or embraced the value of your love.

5. Be gracious to the other person when they don't understand your actions or reactions to something they do as their way of showing you appreciation or affection. As far as possible, try and explain what's holding you back from being able to fully receive their affection. In order to get the breakthrough you seek in this area you'll need to address the conflicting emotions you may feel at such times.

6. Be honest and allow yourself to become vulnerable while taking care. Understand that there is a growth process involved in your learning journey of the act of giving and receiving love.

7. Ultimately, the choice is yours to make right now.

When you choose to forgive someone who has wronged, mistreated or misjudged you for whatever reason, you free yourself. You release yourself from pain, anguish, torment, anger, resentment, distrust, humiliation, and depression that can ensue when all these feelings come together in full force within you. Depression has robbed many of the pleasure of living a fulfilled well-balanced life.

When you forgive someone, you give yourself permission to love and receive love again. You make room for genuine love to begin to flow to you anew. By forgiving someone who has wronged or taken advantage of you, you reposition your mind and heart to be ready to receive and embrace true love. You equip your heart with the greatest gift available to humankind: the gift of true love.

You take on God's loving character. This enables you to better understand the love of your Creator and to express it to others as the occasion presents itself.

The choice is yours now – will you choose to love today and every day?

Will you choose to free yourself from any chains of unforgiveness that may be holding you back from enjoying a purposeful, love-filled, God-inspired life?

Will you choose to forgive yourself for not appreciating or recognising that you are as worthy of receiving love as you are of giving it to others?

This chapter is close to my heart because I too had to learn to release all the hurts and lies that were systematically instilled into my mind all those years ago by someone who I thought loved me for myself, only to realise that they were just using me for their selfish gain.

As a result of this abuse, I wasted many years denying the gift of real love. Not wishing to get hurt again I had momentarily lost faith in the power of true love. Nearly 10 years later I made the conscious choice to not only forgive afresh, but also to release from my life and focus the people who had confused my idea of true love as described in 1 Corinthians 13. By forgiving their past wrongs against me and my family, and choosing to release them, I realised much later that I was positioning myself to embrace the amazing love that awaited me from my new husband Peter. And so in 2002 I chose to open my heart in faith and expectation for better life experiences to begin to unfold in my life moving forward.

Just as the previous damage to my loving heart was inflicted through the passage of time, the healing process has also taken lots of time and faith. Choosing love every day is a work of faith, a conscious choice, and determinedly embracing the present.

# Chapter 11: My True Love: The Answer to Mom's Prophecy

---

Grace for the journey comes through faith in your calling coupled with Divine timing. Though the vision tarry, wait for it.

Dr Jackie Samuels

---

Grace for the journey comes through faith in your calling coupled with Divine timing.

Since being married to Peter for the last 15 years (how time flies when you're in a right relationship!), my view of unconditional love has taken on new meaning. It's rather sad how initially I had a secret fear that Peter might change his attitude towards me, instead of embracing the true uniqueness of his loving acts of kindness and his gentle spirit with confidence. We both needed time to heal from our broken past, and to be patient with one another. It's interesting how God brought two people together from different parts of the world, with a common love and faith language and a need for inner healing through the power of love and commitment.

Although we are quite different we also enjoy some of the same things. Above all is our mutual love for the LORD and Gospel music. We're both in the educational field. Interestingly, we both did our PhD's at the same University, although while Peter was at Reading University we didn't meet! How strange that we'd walk the same campus streets and not meet in the late 90s - early 2000s! Imagine we also attended some of the same Gospel concerts in London, each driving a Volvo car from Reading, shared some mutual friends, yet we still didn't meet until the appointed time! That's the awesomeness of God's divine timing in everything that concerns us!

I'm so grateful that the LORD allowed my Mom to come out of a 5-day coma in Aga Khan hospital's ICU in Nairobi shortly after I arrived at her bedside from the UK, so she could prophesy over me meeting my second husband. She did this from her death bed, just over a year before Peter and I first met. Mom's prophetic final words to me often ring in my head whenever I recall how Peter and I met. She made me promise her that I would say 'Yes' to the next man that would ask for my hand in marriage, even if he was from the land in which I was currently living and studying. She even added, '...*even if he's a man of God*'.

How did Mom ever know that I had been praying for someone who loved the same God I served and loved? I had not shared my heart's desires and especially my prayer spec for another husband to either of my parents or my family members! See how God answers our prayers when we ask Him in total faith, without limiting how He'll make good His promise to give us our heart's desires according to His will!

If you have asked the LORD to provide you with a help-mate, or if you have lost a spouse and wish to be reunited with a fresh start in married life, it's possible that you can have a loving trusting, mutually respecting and nourishing relationship. It's happened to me; I believe it can surely happen for you too.

With what I've learnt throughout my life, now I'm all about seeing and expecting the best for myself and all around me.

It's been a long road, but today I can honestly say that I've finally learnt some hard lessons from the school of hard knocks. I've learnt that 'bounce-back-ability' is necessary in order to get back in step with God's intended purpose for my precious life. I've learnt that when I focus on positive thoughts, positive actions will follow, manifesting positive outcomes.

I've learnt that it's okay to choose to love some people from a distance, like the star of 'The Secret' Lisa Nichols states so wisely. Love them, but don't let them take charge of your life or define you. I've learnt that doing good to others without expecting anything in return is indeed a virtue. Just be careful that you don't become a doormat for someone else to wipe off their dirty feet on you, metaphorically speaking.

One of my favourite life lessons and truths is that I have been equipped with various skills to be an agent for positive change in other people's lives. We all have. When we share good around us, we create a better, happier place for everyone to coexist. That's one of my biggest dreams for our children in this day and age. As a teacher, mentor and life-long learner, my mission is to share with the world the nuggets of wisdom and character building that I learn, in team events, online, in church, schools, and at home. Now as I watch our sons grow into independent young leaders, I pray that they will be good role models in whatever field of work they choose. Their gifts will make room for them. Even as I am grateful to my parents who accorded me the ultimate gift to pursue my musical skills from a young age, I too wish only the very best for our uniquely talented sons. Yes, in whatever you and I choose to do, our gifts will make room for us. Let that be your mantra: to free up those you are called to nurture in order to help them become who they've been brought into this world for.

As we prepare to step into our life's calling and purpose, it's important to address one final stumbling block that keeps many in a battle that's not their portion: fear. Fear of releasing the past, fear of embracing our true individual identity, and the fear of allowing yourself to thrive. How do we overcome fear? Read on...

## Shifting From Fear to Faith

For God has not given us a spirit of fear, but of power and of love and of a sound mind. 2 Timothy 1:7 (NKJV)

We live by the choices we make.

We do have grief and pain, but when we look at life, we are meant to live it by releasing the pain and grief, and choosing to pass on the wisdom we gain through this journey called life to others along our path.

Don't live life by regrets. Choose to speak words of victory over your life. Your inner being is listening and waiting to help you recalibrate the inner chatter. If you're going through a season of testing and need a breakthrough, you can say right now:

'This trial will never defeat me. I will not continue to live like this. I will somehow turn this situation from defeat to victory. I invite the wisdom of God to guide me into my divine path.' By uttering the above words you are making a choice to change your reality.

Whenever we're going through something new in our lives, we constantly have to make some choices. One of the most fearful things we do is to make a choice to take risks in life. If we don't take risks we stagnate and cannot grow into the fullest potential available to us. How does this factor into your life?

Have you been around someone whose health is diminishing and their life expectancy is slowly ebbing away before their very eyes? What's the one thing that comes to the fore? Regret. They start to wish that they had lived the life they were passionate about, a life in which they were brave enough to take risks. Don't let this happen to you.

Take a moment and ask yourself: 'How many of my greatest fears have actually happened?' 'Of all the wonderful things that have happened to me, how many had anything to do with what I feared?'

The truth is that our fears are just our mind's way of trying to protect us from the unknown. Fear is simply false evidence appearing real, nothing more. Fear doesn't have any power or authority over us unless we give it power by feeding it. When we feed our fears then we are drawn to the very thing we feared. Remember this: We attract to ourselves what we think about most of the time. In other words, what we focus on expands. This is why many people have nightmares after they have been watching horror movies, or if they are worrying about a lack of some sort.

For instance, when one is worried about not being able to pay the next month's rent, they might dream of their home being repossessed or the bailiffs coming and serving them notice.

Someone who is scared of dogs may see a huge terrier across the street. The fear of dogs then creates awful movie scenes in their mind. That night the person dreams of being chased by a dog.

## Unhealthy Fear-based Childhood Incident

A related fear-based scenario once happened to me at age 7 or 8.

One day we came home to find some builders in my neighbourhood had dug a pit, ready to lay a foundation for some new houses. At the time I had a very unhealthy fear of deep holes and trenches in general. I believe this stemmed from an earlier near fatal accident when as a two-year-old I'd fallen into a cattle dip. Thankfully there was no water or cattle treatment when I fell in, otherwise my parents would have had a much harder time of fishing me out and getting medical help in time. The story goes that my older brother and sister who were playing alongside me when I fell in the cattle dip rushed to call Mom who fetched me out. We moved from that region shortly after that awful incident. I've never been back to that scene since!

Back to the unhealthy fear incident:

That night after seeing the foundation pit next to our home, I started having nightmares of falling into a deep dark pit with no one to save me or hear the frantic screams. I must have been screaming out loud in fear because on at least two occasions Mom appeared in the room I shared with my older sister, calling my name. On both occasions Mom found me under the bed where I'd fallen from the top of the double-decker. At some point I believe we swapped places with my sister, moving me to the lower-decker after that. It was a long while before the fear of deep holes and heights abated. Meanwhile my parents took to leaving the bedroom light on when we went to bed so as to encourage me that all was well and help me sleep.

If you are going through some unexplained fear, here's what I suggest:

Look back over your life. Track back to your earliest memory of when you first noticed that fear begin to manifest. What was happening in your life at the time? Who else was there? Can you remember words that were spoken, or any actions? Did someone scream at you or physically attack you? Were animals involved (like in my earlier example)? How's your breathing when you start to be aware of the fear gripping you? Do you hyperventilate (i.e. taking short sharp breaths), or do you hold your breath and shut your eyes tight, quietly willing whatever it is away?

This is important: Have you talked to anyone about your fears?

For many years I did not have the guts to talk about some of my fears, mistakenly thinking that if I shared what I was going through I might be ridiculed. This is not the case, my friend. It would be foolish for someone to laugh at you or make light of your fears. What you need is to voice those fears out loud. Address them head-on. When you talk about what makes you fearful, you will no longer feel paralysed when that feeling threatens to swallow up your confidence and peace. You will take back your control when you face your fears head-on.

You deserve to live a life that is free from oppressive thoughts, actions, or stumbling blocks. You deserve to live a life without limits. You were created to impact the world with a specific purpose and design for your life. So make the wise choice to cast away all fear, doubt, and any self-diminishing thoughts that show up in many different forms. Make the choice to live your life to the full extent possible – a life without limits.

The tools you need to impact this world with your voice are already within you. You just need to align your inner voice with your outer reality and you will find that your life will start to manifest everything you need to bring your purpose to the fore.

Remember, delay is not denial. You vision may have delayed, but at the precise moment when it is meant to manifest, it will surely come to pass, and will no longer delay.

Rise and shine! Shine your light all around you! Let others bask in your light as together you bring hope and a brighter world unfolds before you!

# Chapter 12: Where Faith Meets Miraculous Healing

This brings us to an important reality many miss. When you go to the GP with a headache, aching muscles, amnesia, or whatever other ailment, what typically happens? The doctor checks you out then offers some remedy to sort out the symptoms. Meanwhile the root cause of how your body is feeling may be very different to the symptoms the doctor is focusing on or treating. This has happened to me several times. This is why over the last decade I've taken to researching what's going into my body in order to better understand how my body reacts to certain foods, exercises, and daily patterns that I put it through. This discovery has revealed that some sitting positions can cause aches and pains that are similar to what the GP has described as the 'problem' going on within me.

Remember the episode I shared in Chapter 6 on injustice and ill health? I saw the hand of the LORD in giving me resilience to take ownership of my health by seeking a second opinion.

The drastic action I took after this scary incident helped me because I chose to listen to my body, follow my heart, and to do some common-sense research on the primary and secondary effects of the drugs I'd been given. I've often wondered where I'd be today if I had continued taking those drugs...

While I'm grateful for the medical profession and the care they accord patients like myself, this near-death experience taught me a vital lesson: the symptoms and the root of the challenges we face are not the same. The root cause can often be found only when you dig deeper and examine what happened in a particular episode of your life.

The challenge then is to examine past experiences that resulted in a sudden change in direction. Identify something that happened in your life that shifted your sense of security, or created a sense of loss, overwhelm or dependence on something, someone or both. The situation may have been caused by a tragic event that affected you as a child, where certain memories have been deeply buried in the depths of your mind.

Dig deep to discover the root cause of your ailment, simply addressing the symptoms alone will have no lasting positive change. I recently read a powerful quote by T. Harv Eker, author of 'The Millionaire Mind', which helped to clarify something I was mulling over: 'If you want to change the fruit, you have to change the roots. If you want to change the visible, you have to change the invisible first.'

This is so powerful! Many times we're faced with outcomes that are incongruent with what we envisioned for our lives and wonder how they came to be or where we went wrong.

In the following section we'll examine some of the benefits of something that's freely available to each one of us in order to understand how to apply these nuggets to our own lives.

## Chapter 13: Being Aligned to Your Destiny Helpers

Destiny Helpers are the people who are brought into your life to usher you into your divine calling or destiny.

There are both long and short seasons. Some people are assigned to guide you through a short specific season, for instance personal trainers, course supervisors, coaches and mentors, spiritual leaders, among others. In other instances someone may be brought into your life to guide you through a transitional phase where you are perhaps overwhelmed and need emotional, spiritual or other support and guidance through the change. In either case, two or more seasons converge and synchronise in your favour.

You ASK (Always Seek Knowledge) and then you receive your answer. This often happens in an unexpected way; there is no specific formula or pattern as everyone's situation and life experiences are individual to them.

If you look back over your life, you will see a pattern emerging where you prayed one time, in absolute faith, and that one prayer set in motion a pattern that started to bring together a series of doors, people and situations to you. Imagine for instance that you were invited to an interview for a job you'd applied for months prior and not heard anything back for months. Suddenly someone remembered you and put your name forward for the position that was perfect for you. In this scenario you were favoured on the recommendation of others who you may or may not know in person.

Remember the story of Joseph in the Old Testament? He was thrown in jail following a lie that Potipher's wife made up about him when he refused to indulge her indiscretions. After helping fellow prisoners by interpreting their dreams which both came true, the butler promptly forgot about him until 2 years later when Pharaoh needed an interpreter for a series of dreams what were tormenting his spirit. You can read the full account in Genesis chapters 39 through 41. At the appointed time Joseph was set before the king and declared that although he himself could not interpret the dreams, God would give Pharaoh the answer he desired (see Genesis 41 verse 16).

Joseph proceeded to interpret the dreams Pharaoh had and was thus elevated to the person in charge of Egypt, answerable only to Pharaoh himself. Joseph's years in prison were a setup for a comeback, with greater glory and higher standing. Thus we see how God used Potipher and later Pharaoh to usher Joseph to his divine appointment. The passage of time in oblivion was a necessary part of God's plan to show us that He is able to lift up even the lowest among us when we wait patiently in faith and obedience for His divine timing. Have you considered how your trials have been used as a preparation ground for a higher calling?

I've had many Destiny Helpers appear along my path through the years. In this section I'll share four main ones who've clearly been sent to unlock some transitional doors in my current family's lives.

## Destiny Helpers #1: MA, Readjustment After Loss

The first Destiny Helper I'll share with you is my long term friend Mrs Luzili Mulindi-King. Formerly my MA tutor at Kenyatta University, Luzili taught me that embracing a loser's mentality was not going to help me move forward in a male dominated world and culture in Kenya in the late 80s - early 90s. Shortly after my first son was born in 1992 I was invited to attend my MA proposal viva. Upon arrival I was faced with incredible hostility and machoistic attitudes from the predominantly male panel. I was not prepared for the gruelling session that followed, lasting over two hours. I could hear my three week old baby crying agitatedly for his Mommy from the next block. He needed his feed and I was visibly lactating, the evidence of which soiled my top, to my utter embarrassment. The Dean was the only other female in the room filled with at least five males. Her plea for mercy to the male panel to allow me time out to feed my baby who was also in a cast following surgery from a birth defect fell on deaf ears.

In exasperation I eventually burst into tears and the men were bewildered. Up to this point they'd clearly appeared to be thoroughly enjoying my anguish. Eventually they released me to attend to my baby. I later learnt that their questioning and argumentative approach were the mainstay of such Post Graduate proposals and Vivas at the establishment; by this point I was pretty fed up with it all. I headed home and was feeling quite miserable when I appeared for my next lecture with Mrs King the following week. This kind tutor was expecting her second baby at the time. When I responded carelessly to her question without thinking, she pointed out quite calmly that whatever I was feeling beefed about was not of her making or something to that effect. I needed to try and focus on the task at hand in order to make progress in what I was learning in her unit if I wanted to achieve my desired goal.

I took away an important life lesson from our encounter that day. Ultimately what I did and how I reacted to what happened in my world was my choice to make good by turning around the situation to improve my world. The alternative would be to allow myself to be trodden on by others. If I chose the latter option, I would be giving away my power to others who didn't have the best interest for me or my family. Mrs King often invited my son and me to their home which was filled with such love and mutual respect that I began unconsciously desiring positive relationships and experiences for myself. This was a small but significant seed sown in my mind; only time would tell where this seed would end up. I had a choice to either water my seed of hope with love, positive thoughts and actions, or to discard it along with the rest of the bad seeds that seemed to be showing up everywhere around me during that confusing phase of my life.

Luzili sent over from the UK the most beautiful first baby shoes my son ever wore when he was just a few months old. The feeling of warmth and deep gratitude to Luzili's family was tangible for their loving act of kindness, even from such a distance! Another spark of hope was fuelled within me right there and then.

As the decades have passed and our journeys have transitioned, we now live within two hours of each other in England. Luzili broke out in lilting excitement when I informed her of my wedding to Peter in 2003. With great joy in December of the same year of our wedding Luzili travelled from her home near Wales all the way to Reading to witness my PHD graduation, braving the cold rainy Saturday morning to celebrate the special day with us. She also got to meet up with some of our old friends and family. I'm truly grateful for such immense love in action.

## Destiny Helpers #2: Mom's Prophecy Realised

The second Destiny Helper I'll share is my late Mom whose words of prophecy over my life at a time when

I needed to transition into my present reality was the key that set certain events in motion. I've outlined in a previous chapter how Mom's words created my current reality because I chose to receive them and believe the LORD to make true His Word concerning my life. I often still hear Mom's advice ringing in my mind when faced with a dilemma.

Mom would have been proud to see how my life has turned around as a result of her prayer investment and prophetic utterance that unlocked the crucial door that was to be the landmark for my life's turnaround. Indeed, we have an anchor that keeps the soul. Faith has a voice, my voice. Faith, hope and love are the three-way cord that is not easily broken.

I now realise through all Mom endured when we were growing up, that her faith in God kept her grounded on keeping alive what was most important to her – her united family. I've since endeavoured to keep our family together through love, with daily sprinklings of faith and hope in action. The baton Mom passed on to my next Destiny Helpers has helped to complete the healing process in myself, Peter and our sons.

## Destiny Helpers #3: PHD Studies, Mom's Passing, Family Transition

My third Destiny Helpers are my PHD supervisors at Reading University: Professor Paul Croll and Dr Gordon Cox who jointly infused wisdom and persistence strategies that set in motion a pattern that I now live by. I appreciate these two humble champions for their unwavering faith in my musical gifts and passion to contribute towards a path that would create greater and more applicable learning environments for children and young people with special educational needs in Kenya, the UK and the wider world. When my mother was in a coma at ICU in Kenya, my supervisors were quick to offer me all the practical assistance and time I needed to contact my family and arrange my travel back to Kenya before Mom passed on.

Grandma was also ill and had been admitted into hospital months before Mom took ill. She sadly breathed her last the day after Mom's funeral shortly after learning of Mom's demise. Thus we laid two family members to rest six days apart. My supervisors helped me get back on my feet a month later when I returned to the UK after the two funerals, then found myself without a place to stay as my stipend had been suspended while I was in Kenya dealing with these family issues. Adding to this was the urgency to bring my son to join me the UK, necessitating me to move from the halls of residence into private accommodation.

Things escalated quickly when I tearfully shared my plight in church. The LORD provided help from various sources: a single lady from church who had a two bed-roomed house nearby offered me a room while I looked for a more permanent solution for us. The church also blessed us with a love gift to help pay for my accommodation and help settle the balance of

Mom's huge hospital bill. My supervisors also arranged with the University for a compassionate contribution to help with my upkeep for the transitional phase since I was out of pocket for five months. For each of these divine gifts and destiny helpers I am eternally grateful.

## Destiny Helpers #4: 2nd Marriage, Birth of 2nd Son

The forth Destiny Helpers are my favourite relatives and life-long mentors Annie and Sammy Mwangi. I describe this couple as my long season destiny helpers as they've continued to faithfully walk with me and my current family since my teens. As god-parents to my first son, they have availed themselves for every major life event in our lives. For instance, after Mom passed away and my son needed to join me in the UK, they paid for his ticket and organised for his travel. The young lad received VIP treatment on the flight with the air hostesses falling over themselves to make sure he was comfortable. He was also chaperoned by a kind gentleman who played games with him to while the time away. I was so proud of my son for travelling on his maiden plan ride without me!

Another powerful perfect timing of our lives' destiny was directly connected with Mom's prophetic words coming to fruition when Peter and I met. I remember phoning Aunt Annie one day to ask her if I could introduce them to a dear male friend I'd met in church a few months prior. She was intrigued to put it mildly and said, 'Of course; who is he?' Imagine how I was blushing through this phone conversation. We devised a plan of action. Since the previous experience with Dad's disapproval of my late first husband I was reluctant to initially introduce Peter to him. Aunt Annie and I agreed it would be best to first meet my mysterious friend quietly at their home. Peter travelled to Kenya during Easter of 2002 and met them.

Peter must have been keen about me because in July he travelled back; this time he met up with my immediate family including Dad. It seems Dad had mellowed over the years because he immediately took to my tall handsome shy friend Peter. The two became fast friends, and Dad would always ask after his son Peter whenever we spoke on the phone. This bond was making me slightly uncomfortable because I'd learnt to be on guard, so it took some convincing and lots of prayer to finally release my heart to connect with Peter as a friend rather than a Pastor which was really odd. I guess I still had some 'heart baking' to do!

During my wedding to Peter aunt Annie travelled from Kenya together with Dad and other family and friends. 'Mom' Annie and Dad handed me over to Peter with such pride it melted my tender heart. Then when our second son was due to be born and I had a medical emergency that necessitated my stopping work six weeks early, Aunt Annie flew over again to spend the final weeks with me. I remember how we formed the habit of walking nearly 2 miles up the hill to buy wool to knit Baby's first hand knitted cardigan, mittens and hat set. My first son who had also caught the knitting bug produced a fantastic blue and white scarf for his younger sibling to match his Nan's handiwork. His friend also knitted a beautiful scarf for his younger sibling who was born two weeks before our baby. Yet with all those hill climbs Baby was not in any hurry to arrive before his time.

My blood pressure was high and I'd been on insulin for nearly 4 months by the time Baby arrived. I'd grown to the largest I'd ever been with this second pregnancy. When I couldn't walk up the stairs, my hands helped my climb up as I wondered how cats must feel climbing stairs on all fours. Whenever I worried that I wouldn't fit through the door in my size 20/22 (up from a mere 12/14 with a lost pregnancy in between) auntie would jokingly tell me she'd give me a nudge in should I need it.

The night before I went into hospital Peter treated us to the tastiest meal ever at the Outback Steakhouse in 5 Ways, Birmingham. The portions were huge! The brown bread was something else! I wondered if this was to be my final meal before Baby decided to arrive. As it turned out, it was as the following morning I was escorted to the hospital for a long wait before Baby decided to show up. Finally! The lead up to the birth was not without its challenges... that's a whole other story.

To summarise, I went through three epidurals, oxygen and morphine, clamps, the works. To top it off, Baby had to be revived as there was no heart beat when he was born with the umbilical cord tied round his neck and hand. The afterbirth was so stubborn it was nearly an hour after the birth when it finally released itself from my super-tired body. I watched all the drama going on with our baby as I lay helplessly bleeding and trying to remain calm after over 21 hours of labour. Peter did a sterling job throughout, rubbing my back with endless soothing words of encouragement and prayers for Divine intervention ringing through. I was so grateful for Aunt Annie being present to guide us through this tough season. Both my babies' deliveries came with their unique challenges, twelve years apart. Both were incubated for a while. All in all, I'm eternally grateful to the LORD for these two miracle sons.

Uncle Sam travelled to witness our baby Jonathan's dedication. That was two visits from my second parents in ten months. What a blessing! Both families have a home away from home whenever each family visits the other. It's no wonder my handsome hubby loves spending time with his 'Kenyan parents' on his mission work in Kenya!

## Peter Weds Jackie: Highlights

We had an international guest list with family, friends, Gospel artists, Church Ministers and former students. Some of our friends and family had travelled all the way from Kenya, Uganda, India, US and around the UK just to share in our joyous celebration and thanksgiving. This was love in action!

Dad arrived on the same day as my former duettist and co-director Ian who entertained us with some Gospel and African tunes. There was no shortage of musicians to our delight. Aunts Polly and Annie arrived together; we talked deep into the night on the eve to the wedding. I laughed so much at their jokes and stories, being too excited to sleep early. We all had a great time during the traditional 'goat exchange' ceremony a couple of days to our wedding, much to Dad's delight. This is a time when the groom's family meets the bride's family with a special 'thank you' handshake for bringing up their daughter to that point. The best man Jonathan Wordell winged it beautifully as our dear friends Tim and Susan Kanyonji filled in the gaps in expert form.

The night before our wedding a cousin and two former students from Kenyatta University phoned me to ask for the church address. They then said, 'See you tomorrow, Jackie! We're so excited for you!' As I put the phone down, I cried in gratitude, so deeply humbled by the realisation that these precious souls had gone out of their way to change their flight return times just to attend my wedding! And all this time I'd been thinking to myself that Peter would have about 200 people while my side would only boast a handful of family and friends. As it turned out, the LORD heard my heart's desire and chose to bless us with a heart-warming turnout of some of our most special friends.

The guest list turned out to be twice what we'd initially thought, with ample food for all. Apart from my two supervisors gracing our wedding, the Keefes, long term friends and fellow musicians from the British Embassy were also in attendance. They sang one of our favourite acapella pieces, 'Brother James' Air' by J L M Bain. Our bridal party boasted relatives, sons, god-daughters and long term friends.

What can I say for the outpouring of love on every level? Thank you all for attending our BIGGEST day ever, and for granting us your most precious gifts – your presence!

Our 'secret' honeymoon location turned out to be a tour of the South-West of England: Torquay, Penzance, Lands End and the Isles of Scilly. Despite the unpredictable weather we enjoyed some long country walks while watching the beautiful daffodils in St Mary's Island. This was the perfect wedding overall.

Shortly after our wedding we moved to Birmingham where we've made our home.

# Chapter 14: Timing in Showing up in the Now

As with everything in life, there is a right time to show up. Look at the lifestyle of the LORD Jesus Christ of Nazareth.

He was virtually unknown to the world for most of His first 30 years. Yet, for all His living humbly and in obedience to His earthly parents, we are told that Jesus already displayed exceptional leadership qualities. The Gospels record that at the tender age of 12 years the young lad Jesus amazed the teachers of the law in the Synagogue when He interacted with them. The Pharisees only saw 'the son of the carpenter'. Yet Jesus was much more than that – He is the Son of the Most High. His wisdom was not from earthly parents. Yet, living amongst earthly folk Jesus amazed even the wisest among the older teachers at the Synagogue! See how the LORD Jesus' gift was already making room for Him at the tender age of 12 years? His Name was making ripples within the Jewish leadership circles! How cool!

Yet in the final three years of His life the LORD Jesus taught the world LOVE like it had never before experienced! He taught forgiveness of sins when someone wronged another. He taught embracing truth and sharing it boldly. He taught wisdom, peace, and the need to be still in order to recharge one's batteries and seek Higher guidance. These are just some of the gifts Christ gave the world freely. Yet they crucified Him! Notice the words of Jesus as He hung on the Cross? 'Father, forgive them for they know not what they do'. These words have rang in my mind during those trying moments when my lips were too frozen to utter them, as others tried to steal my gifting and silence my voice.

That's how this book came to be written. Two years ago the LORD instructed me to share my life story. Yet I still carried a deep inner feeling of emotional hurt from the painful past experiences I endured. All through this writing process I've been concerned about breaking down as I penned down the worst season of my life. Yet since the start of my writing journey I have come to realise that it's fine to go through all the deeply personal feelings; this is where the completion of my inner healing is being manifested.

It is my sincere desire and prayer that my story will give hope to someone who has been on the brink of giving up and 'tossing it all in the air' so to speak. Realise that your story will empower someone else – only if you are willing, humble and brave enough to share your story and journey in whatever form that is available to you. Just be true to yourself. Allow yourself to embrace the healing that comes from being faithful to your calling. Allow yourself to be vulnerable as that's when you'll discover the hidden pains and confusion that have eluded you for so long, as happened to me. Trust and obey your instinct and willingly let go of the past. It takes a lorry load of courage and a tablespoon of faith to get the first line written down, but it is oh so worth it.

With every word I type I am now truly coming 'out of the ashes and into my calling.' Incidentally this is the title of my new song. Look out for it...

## Find Your Gift and Voice in Every Day Experiences

Let's talk about you for a minute:

What's happening with you? Have you noticed snippets of your gift or uniqueness being manifested in your life? How has it been made evident?

Look back and recall how your spoken words or interactions with others effected change in the environment around you.

Were you chosen to be a school prefect? If so, what were your roles? How about clubs and sporting hobbies you were a part of? Were you in the Church or school choir? Do you play an instrument or engage in public speaking? Are you a good story teller, dancer, poet, singer or fine artist able to describe the world through pottery, paintings, music or sculptures? Are you set to be the next Einstein, Picasso, Michael Jordan, Oprah Winfrey, Tony Robbins, or President?

How are you using your gifts to make room for you?

Has the window of opportunity opened up for you yet? Perhaps you've received invitations to speak at a ladies' or men's conference or been called to share your wisdom nuggets or artistic skill at a youth event. Did you take up the challenge or did you chicken out? Do you feel unworthy of the attention and honour and make up some excuse to not let your little light shine? Don't worry about those lost opportunities to rise and shine with your God-given message to the world. I pray you will get a second chance to make a difference like I did.

The first time I was invited to speak at a Ladies' conference I was surprised that they'd even think to choose me! No number of excuses would get me out of that speaking gig though. In the end when I attended and simply committed to sharing from my heart (having spent ages prepping, fighting to calm my nerves, fretting and all the rest of it) I found that I actually 'tuned in' and rose to the occasion once I got started! And the positive responses from the audience after the presentation only served to bolster my confidence. The immense gratitude I felt at being chosen to make even a small difference in someone else's life was amazing!

This is what could well happen for you once you choose to overcome your shyness, self-consciousness, negative self-talk and all the other limiting beliefs standing in your way. People will line up to hear what you have to say. And the message you are carrying? Only YOU Can Deliver It.

You have greatness within you. You are born with a greater purpose than what you have experienced so far. That purpose is to impact positive change in the world around you - and beyond.

Here's some sage advice to keep in mind when the seed of doubt creeps into your mind:

Refuse to let any outside force snuff out your zeal for life. Refuse to listen to those inner voices that think they are trying to protect you by telling you 'Surely you can't do it. You're too - young, too quiet, too shy, too inexperienced, you slur your words, you don't

---

> Those who choose to acknowledge and receive our gifts are transformed because they chose to connect with us.

have the right credentials or background ... Who do you think you are?'

Let me remind you that whatever they say about you is NOT you. Stop listening to those naysayers! They are only out to steal your dream. I need to say it again:

GREATNESS RESIDES WITHIN YOU.

You only need to tap deep within you to find your calling now. Your calling will show up when you stop listening to the negative noisy voices within you.

You will find your life-giving voice of truth when you are still and make room to listen to your Inner

Guidance. Only then will you start to unleash the power stirring deep within you. You'll begin to push through and step into your greatness, divine calling and destiny.

**Key Takeaway**:

***Our Choices Expand and Guide our Focus.***

# Chapter 15: Empowerment for the Mission Ahead

> Write the vision, wait for its appointed time, tarry and believe the LORD's timing for He will surely bring it to pass. (Paraphrased from Habakkuk 2:2-3, NIVUK)

Write the vision, wait for its appointed time. As you tarry and believe the LORD's timing, He will surely bring it to pass.

We trust in the LORD who is the Promise Keeper. He is also the Way Maker, Miracle Worker, Light in the darkest hour, Tunnel Leader, Dream Completer, Hope, Faith & Honour Restorer, and our Patience Rewarder.

My friend, it's time to Be Excited About Your Life!

I recently read a message that fits me perfectly. The key take was a challenge to be excited about my life. Here's my response to this powerful message:

When we take a back seat to our dream we are bowing to another's dream. Each will stand and be asked, 'What did you do with your talents?'

So my question to you is this: When all is said and done, and the end draws near, you will look back at your life.

Then the Master will ask you with a gentle voice:

'My child, I blessed you with unique gifts. What did you do with them?' The conversation might continue: 'Did you inspire others with your musical gifts? Did you reach out to lift someone up from despair? Did you give back to the community as an appreciation for all the people who invested their lives, finances, talents, time, vision, wisdom and hope in you? OR,

'Did you just dig a hole wide and deep enough to hide your special talent so others would never find it? Did you take it upon yourself to decide that your dreams didn't matter much to anyone? Were you too afraid that others might tag you as being strange for going after your dreams?'

Your dreams matter. End of story. When you choose to obey that persistent voice within you to follow and start living your dream, you give yourself permission to be used to effect the change in your world that you know you are called to. No one else can do what you were designed to do. That book that is incubating within you, that story bubbling inside of you, that speaking engagement that's looking for you right now, that song ringing in your ears and igniting your spirit within – none of these can be told, shared or performed by anyone else other than you, my friend. These are YOUR talents to share with the wider world.

It's time to step into your calling and make a difference.

Imagine walking down the street and someone stops you, excitedly taps your shoulder and asks you, '*Hey! Are you (your name)?*' You reply, '*Yes, I am.*' The person animatedly goes on to recount how you inspired them with your song, poem, motivational video or story. If you hadn't showed up to share your dream that day, that person would likely have given up or their life might have taken an entirely different path. They may never have been delivered from an addiction that held them captive until you came along.

Remember this: What you share with the world will make a difference in someone else's life.

Your DREAMS, Your TALENTS, Your SKILLS All Matter. Share them out selflessly. Give graciously in abundance and expect your numerous seeds to yield a harvest that comes back to you in much more than monetary returns. When we give from the heart, the universe – orchestrated by God the Creator of the universe – goes forth to trumpet our action far and near, sharing our message wherever it is needed and received. Those who choose to acknowledge and receive our gifts are transformed because they chose to connect with us.

## Letting Your Light Shine

You may be suffering from shyness, an inferiority complex, or a feeling that you are not good enough. Do you wonder why God would choose you to be the change agent in your community? Has a word of prophecy been spoken over your life declaring that you will be a world mover of some sort? Perhaps your spirit is not yet in alignment with that word.

Nonetheless, this does not negate the truth of the word spoken over your life. Remember simply that you don't need to know the 'how' of the LORD's promise to you. You just need to accept, embrace the truth, and to ask your Creator to show you, use you, align you, and guide you into your truth. The rest will fall in place in due season if you faint not.

Ask the Holy Spirit to prepare you and connect you to the specific people He'll use to usher in your greatness. Then with an expectant spirit, right standing with the Holy Spirit and by being obedient to His leading, your dream will begin to manifest.

You will find yourself being drawn to certain gatherings, listening to specific podcasts and video trainings, reaching out to specific people of influence to mentor you, and reading certain books. All these actions will empower your mind, ignite your vision and excite your spirit, bringing it in motion to propel you forward towards birthing your dream.

Don't be surprised when you buy a notebook and fill it up with amazing ideas within a short period of time. Writing down fresh ideas that pop into your

> In the same way, let your light shine before others, that they may see your good deeds and glorify your Father in heaven.
>
> Matthew 5:16, (NIVUK)

head in moments of absolute clarity and inspiration is the mind's way of assisting you to realise your dream. Even though your vision has taken a while to be made manifest, believe that it will come to pass, and it will.

Your Dreams Matter! Believe it, Receive it, Activate it, Live it. Only you can deliver the gifts that have been bestowed upon you. Step out in faith and watch as the universe conspires to assist you to bring your gifts to life! Bottom line: Your Dreams Matter!

## God in My Future …

No matter what has happened in my past, it's now time to reclaim my future. I will do this by living in the present. I choose to no longer look back to what I could have changed. Had I tried to change it, would it have turned out any different from what it is now? I don't know. One thing I do know though is that my future has promise for me. Because I believe that, I choose to focus on my present and hope for a better future.

With God on my side I know I'll be a winner!

The Bible has so many truths that ignite my spirit into song. 'God will make a way where there seems to be no way…'; 'Be still and know that I Am God.'

The present is a gift. Choose to embrace it. Live today for today.

As we step into the final chapter, I want to share some awesome quotes that will help put things into perspective when you are having a 'character building day':

'You know you're on the right track when you become uninterested in looking back.'

The people who are meant to be in your life are the ones who will wait patiently for you to heal. [The good vibe]

When the past calls, don't answer. It has nothing new to say. [Genuis quotes]

---

But I am trusting You, O LORD, saying, 'You are my God. My future is in Your hands.' Psalm 31:14-15a, (NLT)

---

# Chapter 16: Don't Take the Safe Path; Push Through into Your Divine Destiny

When you feel yourself reminiscing about what might have been, stop and check yourself.

Don't look backwards for guidance. There's nothing left for you back there. Those experiences have already happened. They are over and done with. If you must reflect on the past, let it be to inform you of what went wrong so you will know how to avoid such mistakes as you move forward in your life journey.

You are no longer that person you were back then. You've moved on and should therefore keep your eyes, mind and sights focused on what lies ahead of you. The journey always moves forward,

never backwards. There are new experiences in store for you so don't look back with regret. Instead, look forward with excitement and anticipation of better things that are yet to be unleashed to you.

Whatever painful paths your past journey took you through have been there to shape who you are meant to become. You are a work in progress. Embrace the new you and give thanks for what the new you is bringing into this universe.

Pull yourself together and focus on the NOW. Focusing on the NOW is so powerful.

Give thanks for TODAY. Give thanks for the people, places, experiences, blessings and joys of TODAY.

Being grateful is the key that unlocks access to the Divine. Thanksgiving is an act of worship to the Creator. Therefore give thanks for being allowed to see this day and smell the fresh air. Give thanks for the opportunity to enjoy the new relationships being availed to you and for the chance make a difference in someone's life today.

There is beautiful healing in being true to oneself. Be true to yourself and to others. Always act with integrity and honesty.

Finally remember that those who choose to acknowledge and receive our gifts are transformed because they chose to connect with us.

# Final Thoughts: You Are A Vessel of Hope

I have now fulfilled the unction to release my past and step into my preordained destiny in order to fulfil all that I was created for. My mission with sharing the deepest parts of my journey is to help every aching soul that is desperate to escape from the guilt and limiting beliefs that the past has dealt you. It is your divine destiny to finally be free from trying to be perfect. Release yourself from the pressure of trying to fit in with everyone else's description of who they think you are or should be, and step into your own path and true worth. Are you ready to release your message and let your light shine for all to bask in its glow? This is your time. Just commit to being authentic and do YOU.

I am excitedly expectant of all the new life changing experiences that await me and everyone who takes the actions outlined in this book. It is my sincere prayer that you will find the grace to forgive others that have wronged you. Also forgive yourself and release the past that can no longer serve you from this point on. Only then will you be empowered to embrace the future that awaits you with a clear and peaceful focus. Step into your divine destiny armed with love and gratitude as your secret keys to unlock the new doors being positioned for you to step through. You are awesome!

# Appendix 1: My Story Shared in Kenyan Tabloids

The tabloids got interested in my story and progress as they learnt of some of the awful experiences I was going through at the hands of my former in-laws. As a national performer my day to day life was not very private. I was interviewed by journalists who attended some of the key national events and performances that I performed in. They retold my story in The Standard and the Sunday Nation papers. Some of my favourite co-performers are Ian Mbugua of the 'Tusker Awards' fame and Carol Ng'ang'a, a fellow colleague of Kenyatta University and distant relative.

The three of us also regularly performed Handel's Messiah at the Bomas of Kenya. Ian and I were also long standing members, soloists and choral leaders at St Andrew's Church Nairobi where we grew our spiritual wings. I was privileged to have accompanied the choir on the piano and organ. My Dad Washington Muuya was also a soloist and composer / arranger of African tunes to Christian lyrics. He did this at a time when there was deep controversy about performing secular melodies in a church context, even with spiritual text. Many Christians initially viewed such songs with suspicion. With the changing attitudes in the Christian arena in Kenya, many of his songs have since been recorded and performed by numerous church-based choirs over the years. Glory to God for sharing His gifts to us so that we can be a blessing to the body of Christ as we enrich one another!

The picture on the next page showcases Carol, Ian and I performing Donizetti's arias, duets, and trios at the Kenya National Theatre to mark 200 years since Donizetti's birth. All the lyrics were in Italian, a very lyrical and engaging language. The performances were directed by Thomas Dilger, music Director at the German School, Nairobi.

The final image shares a deeply moving story recorded by Fred Mudhai of the Daily Nation in 1995 when my son was only 3 years old. I was also interviewed with the outgoing American Ambassador Aurelia Brazeal during the Black History Month festivities in Nairobi. I am reminded to never give up believing and speaking life into dead situations using the tools at my disposal – my music. What's your

> You are my God. My future is in Your hands.

favourite 'pressing on' tool that uplifts your spirit?

The Sunday Nation, May 18, 1997

The singers who performed a wonderful tribute to composer Donizetti. They are, from left, Carole Ng'ang'a, Ian Mbugua and Jackie Muya.— *Picture by JOSEPH MATHENGE.*

# Tribute to Italian composer

### By MARGARETTA wa GACHERU

Celebrating anniversaries of obscure European composers does not usually mean much to Kenyan audiences. But then, the Italian Institute of Culture found a way this past week to create wide-ranging interest in the musical genius of Gaetano Donizetti, the Italian composer born 200 years ago this month.

While many local music-lovers may not be familiar with Donizetti's numerous operas, we are well aware of the elegant voices of Kenyan soloists Jackie Muya, Ian Mbugua and Carole Ng'ang'a. To bring out the beauty, freshness and delicacy of Donizetti's operatic works, particularly *La Lingera, Don Pasquale, Lucia di Lammermoor* and *La Favorita*, the Italian Cultural Institute director, Prof Festa-Farina, invited the three to sing last Wednesday night at the KNT, accompanied by conductor/pianist Thomas Dilger who is also music director at the German School.

The result was heavenly as the three, each singing in solo (apart for Ms Ng'ang'a and Mr Mbugua in a duet from *Lucia di Lammermoor*, and Ms Muya and Mbugua in a duet, *Non fuggir* sang with grace, warmth and appealing freshness.

And while none of them is a native Italian-speaker, they all made it clear why Italian people tend to feel that opera "belongs" to them: Italian is appealingly lyrical.

# 'Music lifts me up'

## Jacqui's father was a musician

ANYONE who has listened to Jacqueline Muuya sing will hardly dispute the fact that the jovial musician is endowed with a wonderful voice. Those who have watched her perform would hardly refute the fact that the Kenyatta University music lecturer prides in enviable personality if not countenance.

Asked how she keeps her voice so smooth and sonorous, she simply says: I take plenty of warm water and lemonade. It is not much wonder that, while addressing guests at the American Cultural Centre — to mark the climax of the recent Black History Month (February), Kenya Broadcasting Corporation (KBC) Chairman,

**By Fred Mudhai**

Dr Gikonyo Kiano and some pleasant words in an allusion to Jacqui's singing a week before at the residence of out-going American Ambassador Aurelia Brazeal.

It is at this gathering of diplomats, Government officials, academicians and university administrators that the writer met Jacqui Muuya - a name that should ring a bell, even if remotely, to many a lover of music.

Singing to keyboard brass by a visiting African-American pianist-duo, Jacqui briefly lifted the guests' spirits with such cherished "Negro spirituals" as *Nobody Knows the Troubles I've Seen* and *Deep River*.

"She has a beautiful voice", Brazeal commented on Jacqui's singing after the show.

Apart from spirituals, her repertoire include classical as well as art or popular songs in both Western and African styles (including folk songs). "My songs and the themes they explore vary according to the occasion" said Jacqui. Fadhili William's famous *Malaika* and Christian song *Ave Maria* are just some of Jacqui's favourites.

The lecturer has also been a music festival adjudicator for nearly ten years. She has adjudicated at various levels from divisional to district to provincial to national in both educational institutions and non-educational institutions music festivals as well as church festivals organised by Catholics and Presbyterian Church of East Africa (PCEA).

### Adjudicator

In this role, she has travelled to Machakos, Coast, Nyanza, Nairobi, Kiambu, Murang'a among other places judging various music categories (solos, ensembles, instrumentals, choral folk songs, dances and marches).

"I have also been invited to adjudicate at private interschool festivals — involving private schools in places like Nairobi", and the chairing singing during a media interview.

Besides teaching music, singing and adjudicating, she also has been a music advisor to various choirs among them Kenya Posts and Telecommunications (KP&TC) with whom she travelled to South Africa where they won trophies and certificates recently.

The lecturer, in her late 20s and a mother of one has also been involved in conducting duties with various choirs among them KP & TC, Kenyatta University, Kenya Conservatoire of Music, Mountgrove, St. Andrews Church and Kenya High School.

It is while at Kenya High School ('77-'82) that Jacqui began participating actively in music. She would be enlisted for solos, duets, trios, quartets and school choirs at the annual Kenya Music Festival. She was the school and chapel pianist and head of the chapel choir.

Little wonder Jacqui emerged one of the two best students in music to university at 'O' Level Kenya Certificate of Education (KCE) examinations 1982. She achieved a similar feat two years later in the 'A' level (KACE)

where she was one of the two highest graders.

In the eighties, the highest scorers in any subject in both 'O' and 'A' level examinations were entitled to some kind of scholarships although Jacqui got none for reasons known to the education possiblities concerned. However, that did not discourage the young and ambitious daughter of former insurance executive Washington Muuya and Muciridicleen ya Wanawake Organization (MYWO) leader Leah Muuya from pursuing her career in music and become a university lecturer. For motivation was from within the family, or rather 'congenital'. The drive was from within the self. It is in-born. It was first nurtured in her rural Kiangoma Village of Mathira Division in Nyeri District.

Her father was an accomplished musician who composed songs in African melodies and gave them sacred text in St Andrew's Church in Nairobi and in the Mountgrove main choir in the seventies.

Even when she decides to take part in drama, Jacqui prefers acting-singing roles especially in musicals like the on-going *The Gondoliers* by Gilbert and Sullivan being staged at Braeburn Theatre where she plays Tessa — one of the principal parts. She has also taken roles in *Oaks and Arrows* by Henry Purcell (in 1985 at Kenyatta University), *Dioego* by Alban Wandago ('90), *"Cadenta's Day"* by Phoenix Players and *Oliver Twist* by Charles Dickens.

### Functions

However, these days she hardly enjoys performing in funerals since they bring her memories of her late husband Ahmed Kipkongri, a former marketing representative with Total Kenya, who was among three work-mates and friends who perished in 1992 in Mukinduri on the Mombasa-Nairobi highway. All the three left behind young widows — one of whom is still Jacqui's close friend, often visiting her thus reminding her that she is not alone in her plight.

She had just sang at the requiem service of a friend at All Saints Cathedral when I interviewed her. "I do not feel comfortable singing in funerals. But I can't avoid it at times", she said, discernibly trying to suppress her emotions.

### Uplifting

"Music is a way of uplifting my spirits through hardships," intimated the mother of three-and-a-half-year-old Edy.

Her Muslim husband, who hailed from Kapsabet, died while she was pregnant with Edy. The tragedy struck three days after her birthday and while she was expecting a birthday gift which the late Ahmed Kipkongri, whom she being forth Edy with a worrying medical complication.

The significance of music to her transformed to that of helping her cope with grief — something that one can seriously discern from the ever-bright countenance. "I am convinced that I hope to pursue my teaching and performing career. I am convinced to teaching others to excel and making others forget their miseries, even if for just a moment", she said in response to a query on her ambitions. "My talent and work is a gift from God, besides being a means of self-expression", the young widow added, emanating noncommittal on whether or not she will re-marry. "Whatever your goals, always strive to achieve them with a positive spirit even in the face of bottlenecks or hardships", she advises the young, thanking all those who have been instrumental in helping her achieve some of her goals.

ON STAGE: Jacqui Muuya as Tessa (2nd lft) with director Sharon Mitchelmore (rt), Stephen Wilson (2nd rgt) and Tom Forster in Gilbert and Sullivan's *The Gondoliers*, which ends tomorrow at Braeburn Theatre.

SING ME A SONG: Jacqui Muuya with out-going American Ambassador to Kenya Aurelia Brazeal during the Black History Month festivities. — *Picture by Jacob Otieno*

## Back to the local entertainment

AFTER shows by visiting Ambassadors Opera from the USA and Alain Kounkou from Paris in Nairobi, "normal" action resumes in the city.

### NAIROBI:

**Pipes:** Double CK productions are on the verge of introducing nyama choma be-rules free music-they offer to revellers.

**Toona Tree:** Calabash Band performs from Wednesdays to Saturdays from 12 p.m. to 4.30 p.m.

**Legacy Africa (Parklands):** Special show from Le Commandant Letana, Sokari, De Bronze and Durose of some tion group Bilenge Musica with lots of African dollars.

**Bond's:** Ileni, Faab, Kivini, Omari and DJ Ronnie have introduced jam session every Sundays from 2 p.m. charges

### WHERE THE ACTION IS

*By Aggrey Kwenda*

at Sha 50 only.

**Solace Hotel:** Music has been introduced at the roof bar at no extra cost.

**Uncle Sam's:** Besides normal live shows by Uhuru Orchestre, host Charles Rajwai has introduced children's entertainment every weekend at no extra charge.

**Wanda Hotel:** (Ruiruka) - Orchestre Beega Africa of Aziz Abdi performs this evening, tomorrow and Sunday free of charge.

**Brilliant Hotel:** Reggae monsters, King Lions are on today from 8 p.m. They re-

turn on Sunday from 6 p.m.

### NAKURU:

**Wayside Hotel:** Simba Wanyika still perform throughout weekend.

### LANET:

**Lanet County Hotel:** DJ Wycliffe Makanga and host Mugo Mathu continue to thrill revellers with their latest hit.

### KISUMU:

**Flamingo:** Experienced DJ Abdallah has re-invaded this town offering the latest from funk, reggae to lingala every weekend.

### MOMBASA:

**Florida:** Offers top selling European and American music seven days a week.

160

Empower your Gratitude journey with your free Download at:
https://bit.ly/GratitudeStarterKitFREEdwnld

For inspirational printables visit:
https://bit.ly/CreativePrintGoods

*With gratitude,*

**Jackie Samuels**

Other books by the author:

https://bit.ly/FamPrayerJournal1

Success Principles for Life:
http://bit.ly/SuccessPrinciples4Life

Join our FB Community:
https://bit.ly/FBThrivingCreatives

Printed in Great Britain
by Amazon